At Break of Day

Gary A. Westgard

ISBN-13: 978-1492991946
ISBN-10: 1492991945

2. Some of the contents of this book have previously been published in:
   (i) *The Journey and the Grace* (Gary A. Westgard/Pine Hill Press, 2007.)
   (ii) A weekly clergy column in the *Watertown Public Opinion*, Watertown, South Dakota, used here by permission.
   (iii) Devotions by Gary A. Westgard for *Christ in Our Home*, Volume 59, Number 2 (Augsburg Fortress Publishers, 2012) used here by permission.

At Break Of Day

Cover photo by Gary Westgard.
Lake Kampeska, Northeast South Dakota, at break of day.

In loving memory
Gunder and Selma Olson
Albert and Beatrice Westgard

In appreciation
Beverly, Merna, Marie

For
Christin and Dean
Joshua and Lilla
Benjamin Magnus and Samuel Finn

and

Vivian
always.

5

Just after daybreak,
Jesus stood on the beach;
but the disciples did not know that it was Jesus.
Jesus said to them,
"Children, you have no fish, have you?"
They answered him,
"No."
He said to them,
"Cast the net to the right side of the boat, and you will find
some."
So they cast it,
and now they were not able to haul it in
because there were so many fish.

When they had gone ashore,
they saw a charcoal fire there, with fish on it, and bread.
Jesus said to them,
"Bring some of the fish that you have just caught."
So Simon Peter went aboard and hauled the net ashore,
full of large fish,
a hundred fifty-three of them;
and though there were so many,
the net was not torn.

John 21:4-6, 9-11

At Break Of Day

Table Of Contents

Life is a gift, a marvelous grace. One way to say thanks is to care for those who share life with us. Jesus has given us a pattern. We are meant to be kind to one another. We are meant to help one another. We are meant to bless one another. My hope, my intention, is that my words will, in a small way, bless you.

Gary A. Westgard
South Dakota, Fall 2013

At Break Of Day

A Morning Word

He has told you, O mortal, what is good;
and what does the LORD
require of you but do to justice,
and to love kindness,
and to walk humbly with your God?

Micah 6:8

A Morning Prayer

Dear God, who made me in the beginning,
be with me this day in all I do and all I say.
Grant me to speak with the kindness of Jesus.
Grant me to do unto others as I wish others would do unto me.
Give me comfort as your child.
Give me courage as your servant.
Amen.

1. I Wish for You, My Grandsons... Old Age

I wish for you, my grandsons... old age.
I wish for you that you feel ache in your bones in the morning,
you begin to forget old friends,
your walk is a bit more unsure,
you have gained some share of wisdom.
I wish for you, my grandsons . . . old age,
for that will mean you have been granted
the unexpected gift of a long life,
days filled with wonder and mercy,
discovering the mystery, the sadness, the joy.

2. The Song of the Bride

When I was a working pastor, I had the privilege of leading worship with many fine musicians. One of the organists would challenge me to tell the congregation to quit visiting before worship. She felt this was only proper, that people looked forward to the quiet and needed the silence. She was not wrong, but I always argued that the sound of the human voice is a good noise, pleasant to the ears, and evidence of people glad to be in one another's company.

This poem reflects my conviction. It is about a community gathering to worship on Sunday morning. I wrote it after leading worship at Zoar Lutheran Church, near Revillo, South Dakota.

The last half-mile is gravel.
The little church sits lonely,
gentle in the morning light.
The door is unlocked.
In the quiet, I put on my pastor garb,
find a bulletin on a table by the door,
a microphone near the altar book.
Then I sit in the front row and wait.
I am waiting for the song to begin.
I will not be disappointed, for soon
a prelude of two voices,
completing the other's verse as they enter.
Then a second couple greeting the first:
How are you today?
How have you been?
A man alone and a family of four,
high and low voices mingled,
soft and loud together: harmony.

17

A family of three,
an old man alone,
two teenagers humming softly.
All join in the song:
Good to see you.
Great game last night.
We could use some rain.
How are the grandkids?
Did you get over your cold?
Glad to be back.
What a beautiful baby.
Verse after verse.
The laughter like a chorus.
The hearty solo of the young farmer,
the melody of women sharing life,
the giggles of children learning the song.
And I, listening from my front row seat,
smile at the beautiful sound,
even as the words are lost
in the building crescendo.
The music of a community,
the song of old friends coming together,
the wedding song of the bride
waiting for her groom to appear.
On the hour, the bell sounds
from somewhere outside
and silence breaks in.
The silence too is part of the song.
Faith is the song.
Love and hope are the song.
In the name of the Father,
and of the Son,
and of the Holy Spirit.
The song continues.
The organ begins to play.

3. When Something Breaks

The sign that marked an acre or more of deserted cars promised, "If it's broke, we can fix it."

I remember the time I bought a long florescent light bulb to replace the old one, which had burned out. I took the old bulb along to the store as something to match the new one against. Returning, I drove into the garage, got out of the car, took one bulb in each hand, turned, tripped, and dropped one of the bulbs. I would not be remembering or telling this story, had I dropped the old burned-out one. That new bulb would not be fixed – not even by the self-assured guy who made promises about old cars. Some things cannot be fixed.

I have spoken words to people in anger, and it was as if I had dropped that new florescent light bulb. Something broke, and it would not be fixed.

Forgiveness is real, but not magic. It will not change the past or erase the memory. Forgiveness says, "I am sorry for what I have done, and I ask you to love me even though I know, and you know, I have done this terrible wrong to you."

Forgiveness can heal, but there is no guarantee that either party will forget. Some things cannot be put back together again.

Forgiveness is no excuse for bad behavior. We are responsible for the words we speak, for the lives we live.

In his Small Catechism, Martin Luther's morning prayer includes this petition: "...protect me today from sin and all evil, so that my life and actions may please you."

~

19

4. Ministry

My second call was to South Dakota, to the two-point parish of Gayville Lutheran, in the town of Gayville, and Bergen, in the country south of Meckling and west of Vermillion. Our children were born in 1970 and 1972, and we lived in the Gayville parsonage from 1973 to 1980, so this is the first home they remember.

Walt and his wife owned and operated a small grocery store in Gayville, stocked with the essentials and some extras, like lutefisk that came in barrels, packed in dry ice. Walt and his store were a gift to the community. Walt trusted us. His charge account consisted of a notebook with your name and the amount you owed printed in Walt's hand.

Walt told this story about himself: In the middle of the night, a woman called frantically, needing something from the store. She didn't tell Walt what it was, but could he please open up the store. He got dressed, drove to the store, unlocked the door, turned on the lights, and waited at the counter as she walked to the back. He thought of all the things she might need: medicine for an upset stomach or headache, milk for the kids, maybe a loaf of bread. She came to the counter and asked Walt to add the item to her account. She walked out the door with one roll of toilet paper.

Walt had a ministry. His altar was that counter where we laid down our offerings, where Walt took an accounting. He accepted what we had to offer, helped us when we needed help, treated us with respect and kindness.

Some clergy and churches do less.

~

5. No Room in the Inn

there is no room
the inkeeper said to the young parents
no room for you
Cain said to Abel
before he clubbed him to death
the Nazis said to six million Jews
as they entered the shower rooms
whites said to blacks
on the way to school
the rich say to the poor
the straight say to the gay
the Christian says to the Muslim
the Muslim to the Christian
the children of immigrants say to those
running across the border
so their children
might say it
when there is still no room

6. Blocking the Cookie Table

I had volunteered to bake and serve cookies at the library, in celebration of National Library Week. There was no expectation of a large crowd, so I brought four-dozen cookies.

The cookie table was set up near the door so that people could see it when they entered. The day passed and the four-dozen cookies looked to be enough. Then, in the late afternoon, a large group of children got off a bus. They were coming for story time. I knew there would not be enough cookies for a busload of kids. I also knew the library staff would serve treats after story time, so as they came in, I stood in front of the table. They didn't see the cookies.

Later, on the way out, the children passed the table again. But this time they stopped at the front door to wait for the bus. They waited a few feet away from the cookie table. It didn't look good and it didn't take long. One of the children moved closer to the table. Two more followed him. I took a step forward, blocking the table. The first child kept coming.

I finally said, "I am very sorry, but we don't have enough cookies for everyone."

He replied in his four- year-old voice, "That's OK, I only want one."

That little boy was not asking for much. "I only want one." Despite all the things we can do—phones that take pictures, instant communication, weapons that can destroy a city in a few minutes—we can't seem to figure out how to make sure that every child has enough food every day.

In Matthew 14:13-21, we are told that when a crowd gathered to hear Jesus speak and it got to be lunch time, the disciples wanted to send people home. Jesus said, "You give them something to eat." (v. 16)

The task seems overwhelming. The reasons for world hunger are complicated, and maybe you and I cannot fix it.

But I can do something, and you can do something, and your congregation can do something.

And you and I can remind our church leaders and our political leaders to do something. John Templeton (1912-2008) said, "If we had been holier people, we would have been angrier oftener."

According to Bread for the World, 925 million people worldwide are hungry. Every day 16,000 children die from hunger-related causes. That's one child every five seconds. Bread for the World contends that we have the ability and the means to produce enough food to feed the world, but we lack the will.

In another telling of the story of Jesus feeding people (John 6:1-13), there is a child in the story, who has brought his lunch of five loaves of bread and two fish. The disciples bring the child to Jesus, but he doesn't seem to understand the math problem. The disciples however do, and they explain the problem to Jesus:

"What are they among so many?" (v. 9)

Jesus never answers the question.

He simply begins to do something.

~

7. After the Funeral

Frank was almost fifty-nine when he died. After the funeral, I told his wife, Ruth Ann, something she already knew: it will be hardest for her. The rest of us will go home, back to routine, back to work and family, back to the familiar, back to the way it was. But for Ruth Ann, it will never be the way it was.

I get weary of the easy words we too often speak at funerals, telling family members it will be okay, or that he or she is in a better place, or "we are here for you." The truth for Ruth Ann is that it will not be okay. Frank will not be around to listen as she tells of her day at work. He will not walk his daughters down the aisle or hold his grandchildren. Frank and Ruth Ann will not do the things they planned to do when they retired.

Most of us, most of the time, like this place called earth. We have gotten rather used to it. That "better place" we talk about is not a place we wish to go to just yet. Frank didn't really want to go to that "better place" just yet either. He enjoyed life; he loved to teach and was good at it. He was interested in many things and was not afraid to share his opinion on politics and the affairs of this world. He cared about people and was open to new ventures. A few years ago he even became a clown. He loved his family and the church. He loved "this place" called earth.

He loved life.

Vivian and I strive to keep in touch with Ruth Ann and her daughters. We send our Christmas greeting and call once in a while. But the truth is, most days Ruth Ann is on her own. After the funeral, friends went home. A few days later, extended family members went home. Eventually even their two daughters went back to their work and homes. Ruth Ann is alone. But she is not helpless. She will endure. She will laugh once again.

Life is precious. Each day is a good day to wake up in this place. The husband who snores too loudly, the wife who buys too many shoes, the kids who give good cause to worry, the family and friends who may become a burden—are all precious.

This morning I got to drive down a street lined with trees dressed in their new fall colors. I had time with my wife, received an email from our daughter, and talked on the phone with our son . . . simple and profound joys.

After the funeral, Ruth Ann told me that we must have hope. It would be even more difficult to go on if she did not have such hope, a hope that is grounded in the words of Jesus who promised to go ahead and prepare a place for us, where every tear is wiped away and death will be no more.

A promise and a hope…

After the funeral, it is what we have.

~

8. So Just Who Decided?

I have come to count on him.
Every Friday he shows up, no matter the weather,
to gather all the garbage that is mine,
take it to a fiery heap outside of town, burn it away.
Like on Sunday, when my sins are gathered up.
So just who decided this man is worth less than the
man who sits behind a large desk,
wearing his silk ties and brilliant shoes,
writing memos, sending out people,
meeting over cocktails,
taking off early on Friday
to play a round of golf?

9. The Healing Power of Licorice

Lucas is still of an age when it is okay for a boy to cry –
especially when he falls down and scrapes his knee, which is
what he did one day not long ago. I happened to be outside (we
are neighbors), and so I heard his cry. I walked over to see if I
could help, as did his two older brothers.

We all asked, in unison, are you okay? Did you hurt your
knee? We could plainly see that he had, but we asked anyway.
His mom came out, picked him up, hugged him, looked at his
knee, and asked if he wanted a Band-Aid®. He was still crying
when I asked, "Would you like a licorice?"

At the word 'licorice', he stopped crying. Immediately. He
looked at me and nodded "Yes."

Ah, the healing power of licorice.

I am not recommending licorice in place of Mom's holding
and hugging, nor in place of a Band-Aid. But licorice can help.
When I asked Lucas if he wanted one, I was saying: "I care
about you."

Recently Vivian and I were in Silver Spring, Maryland,
babysitting our two grandsons for a few days while Mom and
Dad were out of town. The boys were still in school and each
day the four of us walked the half mile there and back together.
One morning it looked like it might rain, so I suggested we drive.
Finn, who is now seven, said, "No, let's walk. I like to walk and
talk."

When he is 'walking and talking' with his Grandma or his
Grandpa for that half mile, he has our full attention. No
television blaring in the background, no newspaper in front of
my nose, no video game tempting him to "come, play."

Just two people sharing lives.

To say to Finn, "Would you like to walk to school today?" is
like saying to Lucas, "Would you like a licorice?" It is a small,
small thing, yet it says, "I care about you".

It is how Jesus spent his life. It is what still attracts me to
him.

27

The stories of his raising the dead or walking on water or changing water into wine only confuse me because they seem so far away from what I have experienced in life.

But those little scenes, those brief encounters with ordinary people who were considered of little value or importance, still encourage and invite me.

Read again the story in John 4 where Jesus stops at Jacob's well and has a conversation with one of the women who has come there for water. Life has not been good to her. She has been married five times and is now sharing her bed with a sixth man. Jesus begins with the simple words, "Give me a drink."

He could have been saying, "Would you like a licorice?" The words stop her. She listens. There is conversation. There is healing.

Or read the story in Luke 7 about the time when Jesus went to a town called Nain. As he was entering the town, a funeral procession was leaving. We are told that the man who had died 'was his mother's only son, and she was a widow.' In other words, she had just lost her livelihood. Without a male in the house, whether father, husband, or son, she would soon be poor and she would remain poor for the rest of her brief life.

As I did for Lucas, so Jesus did for the widow. "When he saw her, he had compassion for her and said to her, 'Do not weep.'" Jesus goes to the body of the dead son and says, "'Young man, I say to you, rise!"

There was a large crowd with that widow and when Jesus did what he did, when he changed reality, when he brought forth life out of death, we are told this about the crowd: "Fear seized them all." They proclaim Jesus to be a great prophet and can't wait to get home and tell the neighbors. The people are astonished by the miracle, but they miss the ordinary compassion that we can all practice. They had forgotten about the mother.

In the middle of this scene, which prompts fear in the hearts of so many, there are these remarkable words: "…Jesus gave him to his mother." This story is not about the son. This story is not about raising the dead.

This story is all about the mother, about returning her son to her, so she can live. This story is about Jesus' compassion for this woman.

And each and every one of us can be in touch with, and can respond to, that part of the story.

The Christian Church is not growing in this country. Members are leaving and young people are not joining. For many, the Christian Church is irrelevant, and maybe boring. It has nothing important to say, and when it does say something good, often the actions of the church do not match the nice words.

But people are still attracted to Jesus. We like what he says and we like how he treats people. He was always leaning towards inclusiveness. He was always opening his arms in welcome to those whom the religious folk wanted to keep out. He was never boring. He noticed people and he paid attention to people. He was doing something all of us can do.

And I would like to think that I was doing something Jesus would do when I went to Lucas and asked, "Would you like a licorice?"

Ordinary, common, everyday compassion.

~

10. Cheap Gas and Keeping the Faith

It happened at a small gas station in Minnesota a few years ago. A man filled his car with gas, paid at the pump with a credit card, and discovered he paid just 27 cents for a gallon of gas. He called a friend, who drove over and filled his car at 27 cents a gallon. He, in turn, called a friend, and so it continued. After some time, a radio station was called, a crowd gathered, the neighbors complained, and the cops showed up. The police finally called the owner of the station. It seems the poor man had set the computer wrong. He meant to set the price at $2.79, but he punched a wrong button.

My guess is that none of those who paid 27 cents a gallon for gas that day would go into a station, pull out a gun and rob the owner of $50, which is about the amount each person saved when he or she put in twenty gallons of gas. My guess is that no one really believed gas was selling for 27 cents a gallon that day, not unless they had been in a coma for forty years or had been stolen away by wolves at birth and had just escaped. When I was at Luther Seminary, I could buy gas for 25 cents a gallon, but that was in 1967.

No, my guess is that every single person who drove to that gas station went there with the knowledge that a mistake had been made, and intended to take advantage of it. They were finally going to 'get back' at those big oil companies.

But no one got back at big oil.

What happened was that some guy in Minnesota, trying to run a business and make a living, lost $1,500, because he punched the wrong button on a computer, and no one had the integrity to tell him that maybe a mistake had been made and that he might want to check his pumps.

How do we conduct our lives when no one is watching?

I once read about an experiment, a study of human nature, conducted in a public restroom. The study found that we are less likely to wash our hands if no one is in the restroom with us.

In the book of Matthew, chapter 6, Jesus says it is easy to practice the faith—easy to be pious—when others can see us.

But God desires to bless in the secret times, when no one but God can see us doing good things.

We sing "Jesus Loves Me" on a Sunday morning, surrounded by others, and feel all cozy inside. We smile at the preacher and smile at one another. We have Jesus in our hearts. But most of life is lived outside the sanctuary, separated from the community that returns our smile. Most of life is lived in the home, the workplace, and on the playing field, away from our cozy place of worship.

What then?

What happens when we must choose between faithfulness and something like cheap gas, and no one is watching?

~

11. God's Dusty People

Actor Woody Allen once said, "I don't want to achieve immortality through my work. I want to achieve it through not dying."

In the Christian faith we begin the season of Lent with Ash Wednesday. On that day Christians gather to have ashes marked on their foreheads and hear words based on Genesis 3:19: 'Remember that you are dust and to dust you shall return.'

We are God's dusty people.

You walk on a beach next to the water and turn to discover that the ocean has come in, gone back out, and taken away your footprints... as if you had never been there.

A favorite movie of mine is Yankee Doodle Dandy (1942), with James Cagney playing George M. Cohan.

Cohan was a superstar of American show business—an actor, singer, dancer, songwriter, playwright, director, and producer—who lived from 1878 to 1942. He was the father of American musical comedy, known from coast to coast, the only actor to receive a Congressional Gold Medal (presented in 1936), and the only actor honored with an eight-foot bronze statue in Times Square.

When my wife was telling a friend about the movie, the friend said that she had never heard of George M. Cohan. Then she went on to admit that she had never heard of James Cagney.

So much for fame...

Psalm 103:14 sings: "For God knows how we were made; he remembers that we are dust."

Take courage. You are remembered. God knows how faint of heart you and I are, and how afraid, we dusty ones. Go out to the cemetery, walk among the stones, and dare to believe.

God says, "I will remember you, even after your life on my earth is over. But now, in your time, consider what you can do with your one life in this often-troubled world. Neighbors all around."

12. Maybe Basketball is Kind of Like Life

I was visiting with Kali, one of the young women on the Watertown High School basketball team. They had won the right to go to the state finals. I attended the game in which that was decided and experienced the excitement of watching this team win. The next day at church I told her of the tension we felt as we watched them play, and I asked her how she and the other players felt. What goes on in your mind? Do you get excited?

Kali replied, "Oh, we are just terrified."

What remarkable insight. Of course we are terrified.

We are the mother who leaves her baby with a sitter for the first time or who drops off her five-year-old at school in the fall. We are the father teaching his son to drive or walking his daughter down the aisle. We are the wife sitting in the waiting room, looking at the clock and the door leading to the surgery unit. We are the one who answers the phone in the middle of the night. We are the daughter visiting the nursing home every day or the son making arrangements at the funeral home.

There is reason to be terrified.

There are many passages in the Bible exhorting us not to be afraid, from the word of God in Genesis, spoken to Abraham as he builds a nation, to the angel appearing to the shepherds in Luke's gospel, to the assurance given by Jesus to the disciples terrified by a storm: "Take heart, it is I; do not be afraid." (Matthew 14:27)

But can our feelings change with a word? If you ask me to climb to a very high place and look down and tell me not to be afraid, my terror will not convert to fearlessness simply by your words, no matter what you say.

When our teenage daughter drove from Vermillion to Sioux City for the first time with a car full of girlfriends, we did not go from worry to sweet serenity just by reminding ourselves that we are people of faith and God is with us. We worried.

Kali, I believe, understands something very important.

Yes, we are terrified.

There are all those people watching; family and friends, and the fans are counting on us. The dream may not become reality; we may lose. But we will trust. We trust our coach, trust our practice, trust one another on the team, and trust the ability that God has given each one of us. So we will do the best we are capable of doing, work as hard as we can work, and we will trust. We will play, terrified and hopeful and confident, all at the same time.

There is a freedom that comes when we own up to our fear. Such a confession creates community, for one such truth telling enables another person, and yet another, to also acknowledge his or her fear, and thereby a strong foundation is set down. Each one discovers that he or she is not alone.

Fear can also be a good thing. It will keep one shooting free throws long after practice is over. It will cause a father to spend extra hours in the car next to this child who begs to drive. Fear will even make a parent brave enough to ask, "Who is going to be at the party and when are you coming home?"

What we learn from Kali is that when Jesus tells us to not be afraid, he is telling us to play anyway, in the midst of the terror. We will drop our children off at school, teach our sons to drive, watch our daughters head off to college, visit our parents in the nursing home, and play the big game. Not because we are fearless, but because we are called to responsibility. And we trust.

Words do make a difference. "Take heart, it is I; do not be afraid," is not meaningless. Faith counts. If we have taught our children well, we trust that such teaching also counts for something. As does community – whether it is family, friend, congregation, or support group; we are not alone. Finally, we dare to trust that God will grant us the courage and wisdom to do what needs to be done, hard as it may be, difficult as it looks. We can do this. We, who are terrified and hopeful and confident, all at the same time...

34

13. Where Did I Put That, And What Was Your Name Again?

It was embarrassing. I was working on a small project and needed to take a painting to Brookings, in order to get prints made. This was all new to me, so I wrote down everything I thought I needed to ask the printer, and I decided to take my cellphone, just in case I needed to call home.

I headed out the door at 9AM with list and phone in hand. I told Vivian I would stop at a gas station, then the bank, and be on my way by 9:30. I would be home by noon.

I was back home at 10:15.

I had filled the car with gas, stopped at the bank, left town on schedule, drove fifteen miles south, and realized I had forgotten to put the painting in the car.

I play a game with my daughter. She will turn to an old movie on television and ask me to identify the film. More often than not, I am able to name the movie, identify some of the actors and the director. Why is it possible for me to name the actors and directors of forty-year-old movies, but I can't remember the name of the guy who is coming over to talk to me at church?

I lament the fact that I have misplaced whole chunks of my life. To recall moments from long ago and to bring back old friends who touched our lives is a blessing. To lose that gift is tragic.

There is a prayer in the Old Testament called Psalm 71. It is the prayer of an older person. Here are two of its petitions:

"Do not cast me off in the time of old age; do not forsake me when my strength is spent." (v. 9)

"O God, from my youth you have taught me, and I still proclaim your wondrous deeds. So even to old age and gray hairs, O God, do not forsake me, until I proclaim your might to all the generations to come." (vv. 17-18)

God has a poor memory for old sins, but a good memory for old sinners.

14. A Prayer for Devon

I have three younger sisters and Merna, the middle one, called.

"I have some terrible news."

In that moment, all kinds of possibilities came to mind, all of them painful.

"Devon was found dead in his apartment."

Devon is the son of the youngest sister, Marie. Devon will be forever 29. Marie called Merna, who called me and their older sister, Beverly. So we all knew, and we all wish we had never heard such news. I asked what happened. She didn't know.

Marie will never get over it. She will never "get on with her life," as we say. Devon will never marry, never be a father, never do all the things we take for granted each day.

There will be all sorts of words spoken to my sister in attempts to comfort her, to help her get through this. But one does not get through this. I will call her soon, and I hate the thought of it. I, too, will try to say words in order to be of help, but they will be as empty as the other words already spoken to her by good friends and family. Everyone wants to help, wants to make it better, but there are no words that seem to be enough. Everything I can think to say sounds false.

I am a pastor. I should tell her about Jesus. But before I am a pastor, I am a brother, her big brother who made things better for her when she was little. When she was born I was thirteen, so I watched over her, protected her, taught her. She told me once that whenever I am around, she becomes the baby sister again.

Another pastor will visit Marie. He will tell her about Jesus and about Easter, but I hope not too soon. We must weep and curse God first, for the senselessness of it all, and for the truth of Devon's absence from this world. To tell of the promise of resurrection and of heaven too soon is to deny the terrible pain of his leaving. Even the one who is called the Resurrection and the Life wept when his good friend Lazarus died.

Let the story of Jesus be told, but not too soon, and do not ask that the story of Jesus take away the agony. To do so is to forget how much a mother loves her child.

The hope of Easter is a hope that can rest alongside the pain, but it will not erase it. Both can be real: the promise of heaven and the sadness of separation. But the sadness is always there, the pain never far away. The promise is like a faraway place one can almost see, almost touch, but not quite. It is like a good dream, but one awakens in the middle of it and finds there is still the truth of what has happened.

Devon is dead. Too soon, he will become a memory, and my sister does not want a memory. She wants Devon.

Oh, my sister, if only I knew what to say.

~

15. The Saddest Words of Tongue and Pen

Only two runs. One game, that was all.

But it didn't happen. The team could not produce those two runs. They could not win that one last game. So the Chicago White Sox went on to play another day and the Minnesota Twins went home to watch and wonder what might have been.

These are familiar words from John Greenleaf Whittier (1807-1892):

For of all sad words of tongue and pen,
The saddest are these: It might have been!

I remember when the Minnesota Vikings were three points away from going to the Super Bowl. One of the best kickers in the game needed only to kick a field goal. It was an almost sure thing. He missed.

God loves us, forgives us, guides us with his Word, gives us hope for our future with his promise. But God will not change our past. Faith is not magic. So we will settle in and live with what might have been.

The prayer of confession we speak in public worship or whisper in the quiet of our room is not only about listing the wrongs we have done and the hurts we have caused. It is also about letting go of what might have been. It is a most difficult task.

We may have faith enough to let God forgive us. It is not so easy to forgive ourselves. Nor is it possible to forget. For sure, remembering can be a good thing. If we forget easily, we may, too soon, repeat our foolishness. If we let ourselves off the hook with a simple shrug, our prayer rings false.

I live with many regrets, but I also trust that I am loved by those who know me as family and friend. I believe God desires me to learn from my regrets about what might have been.

There is no perfection in us. When Vivian once asked why I decided to do "this" when the day before I had decided to do "that," which was just the opposite, I replied, "You must remember that I am a living, breathing contradiction."

We will continue to make decisions that leave us wondering later: "What in the world was I thinking?" We will miss opportunities. We will not always fulfill the expectations placed upon us by others, or even by ourselves.

Regrets come with the game. We will not always hit it out of the park. We will, too often, fall short by one game or by two runs. But I still like the Twins. I enjoy their joy, like children when they win, and I feel sad in their loss. That's what fans are for.

You have your fans: family members who weep with you and cheer for you, and friends who pay attention and are still your friends when you come up two runs short. Family and friends still care. God still loves. Such a grace keeps us.

But God will not change your past.

Settle in and live with it. Know that the past will not destroy you, nor will it stop you from getting up tomorrow and doing the best you can. Allow regret to be that hard teacher. You learned something. Use it.

Life is messy and confusing, even for those who live by faith. God's Word is story and comfort and promise, not a detailed road map and weather report and horoscope. Tomorrow brings with it more decisions, more choices, and perhaps some regrets. Once again you may be left to wonder what might have been. But you keep playing, doing the best you can.

Former baseball player and philosopher Yogi Berra reminds us: "When you come to a fork in the road, take it."

~

39

16. The Right to Go On Living an Ordinary Life

The largest ghetto uprising of World War II took place on April 19, 1943. Hitler's army had invaded Poland in the fall of 1939 and after three weeks of resistance, Warsaw surrendered. There were about 300,000 Jews in Warsaw to begin with, but thousands more Jewish refugees soon came in from smaller towns. In October of 1940, the Nazis announced the establishment of the Warsaw Ghetto.

A wall was built around a section of the city, twenty blocks by six blocks. All Jews in the city were given a month to move into the ghetto, while all non-Jews were ordered to leave.

Conditions were horrible. The elderly and the children died first. Eventually, small resistance groups began to pop up in the ghetto. In the summer of 1942, the Nazis began deporting Jews from there to the concentration camp in Treblinka. From July to September, more that 300,000 Jews were deported, leaving about 50,000 people in the ghetto. When news leaked back to the ghetto of the mass murders, the resistance groups became better organized, making grenades, bombs, and mines, and creating a chain of tunnels and bunkers where the people could hide.

In January of 1943, ghetto fighters opened fire on German troops as they tried to round up more people for deportation. The Nazis were forced to retreat. Then on April 19, 1943, the first day of Passover, hundreds of German soldiers entered the ghetto in rows of tanks, planning to destroy the ghetto in three days. The resistance held on for almost a month, but the revolt ended on May 16 and the remaining Jews were either shot or sent off to concentration camps.

Irena Klepfisz, author and teacher, was two years old during the Warsaw Ghetto uprising. Her father was killed on the second day. On the forty-fifth anniversary of the uprising, Irena Klepfisz said: "What we grieve for is not the loss of a grand vision, but rather the loss of common things… the right to go on living…an ordinary life."

To live an ordinary life is all that most people ask. There are the tyrants and the bullies, the narcissists and the greedy who must be denied, but most of God's children ask only the right to go on living with a sense of purpose and self-worth. Jesus called it the Kingdom of God. To have some understanding of how it works and how it feels, hold a baby in your arms.

~

17. The Kingdom of God
Looks Something Like This

Note: I wrote this piece a few years ago. The boys are older now, but are still neighbors, except for Trevor and Jesse who have moved into another home. Joe is now a part of the community; he greets me whenever he sees me, like we are old friends, and we are. There is also a new baby brother, Lucas, who usually talks to me in long sentences, which I am unable to understand, but it sounds like friendship.

Jacob is five years old. He lives in a home just to the south of ours, and we have lived in our house for four years, so Jacob has known us for most of his life.

His Mom tells of staying in a motel with Jacob. After they got settled in their room, voices could be heard coming from the hallway and other rooms, and Jacob wondered about the voices. His mom said: "Oh, that's just our neighbors."

So Jacob asked: "Are Gary and Vivian here?"

To the north live Josh and Andrew, and across the street are Trevor and Jesse. The five boys range in age from three to eight. Trevor, the eight-year-old, once reminded me, when I got him and his younger brother confused, that it would help if I remembered that he is the older one because he is the taller one. He was right, of course. It does help. I have not mixed them up since.

There is also Joseph, Jacob's younger brother, but he was born more recently and basically spends his time sleeping and eating.

But the other five are out and about. They seem glad to see me, greet me with a wave and a smile. Sometimes they stop to visit, to show off a bike or other mode of transportation, and are a valued part of my life in the neighborhood. Of course, I am not responsible for their food, clothing, shelter, and discipline, so there isn't much to spoil the joy.

This past week my mower quit, so I went to Jacob's Mom and she gave me permission to use their mower. Being mechanically challenged, I could not get the thing started, so Jacob's Mom got Josh and Andrew's Mom, and together we started the mower.

Andrew is three, the fearless one in the bunch. He gets in trouble because of it. He will cross the street without needing a good reason, going where angels fear to tread with a smile on his face. Josh has to watch out for Andrew. Sometimes I do, too.

I think the world is supposed to work the way it works with me and Jacob and Josh and Andrew and Trevor and Jesse. We are neighbors and we look out for each other. I am glad for their joy, glad when they show off a new toy and when I hear them laugh, glad that their parents love them. These parents, of course, have primary responsibility for the greater task of making sure these lovely boys grow up to be good men. But I also have responsibility for their wellbeing.

Christian social reformer Pandita Ramabai (1858-1922) wrote: "People must not only hear about the Kingdom of God, but must see it in actual operation, on a small scale perhaps and in imperfect form, but a real demonstration."

~

18. Sanctuary

The word sanctuary has three meanings:
1. A place set aside for worship of God.
2. A place of refuge or protection.
3. A place where birds or animals are sheltered.

Sanctuary is what the church, the local congregation, can be: a place to worship God, a place of safety and shelter. All are welcome to come into the sanctuary. We read in the Bible about Jesus eating with "sinners and tax collectors" and welcoming children and women, who had no status in society. At table with Jesus was Thomas the doubter, Peter who denied being one his followers, James and John who each wanted to be his favorite, and Judas who betrayed him.

They all ate together.

We need a place of safety, a place where we are not judged on our clothing, or our status in society, or our past. A place where the banker has conversation with the kid who mows lawns, where the executive has coffee with the guy who got laid off from his construction job three weeks ago, where the farmer and the teacher, the waitress and the nurse all feel right at home, and all kneel at the same altar. A place where both men and women are honored, and children are treated with kindness; a place where the newcomer is as comfortable as the eighty-year-old who has been coming since childhood; a place of shelter from all that comes down upon a person during the week; a place where one can come in and rest awhile, before going out again.

If a church is a place where people feel afraid or unwelcome, then it is not Christ's church. If a church is a place where some are given more honor than others, then it is not Christ's church. If a church sets up barriers so it feels more like an airport, then it is not Christ's church. If Jesus is not talked about or sung about, if God is not worshipped or prayed to, if sins are not forgiven or the cross proclaimed, then it is not Christ's church.

44

If the church is indeed the body of Christ, belonging to Christ and obedient to Christ, then the church will look and act like Christ. If I am a stranger, I will be welcomed. If I am lonely, someone will be glad to see me. If I am a kid, someone will give me a smile and a handshake, and say: "Good to see you."

If I need to pray, this place will encourage me. If I need to talk, someone will listen and not judge. If I am a sinner, in this sanctuary I will find forgiveness. If the supper of our Lord is served, I will be invited to come to the table, because it is Christ's table, his church, and his sanctuary.

~

19. Stuff

Vivian and I held a rummage sale recently, and once again I was confronted with this sad truth: I have a difficult time getting rid of stuff.

My stuff, not her stuff...

I have no problem selling Vivian's stuff, but leave my stuff alone.

Vivian contends that we spend the first half of life accumulating stuff. As somebody once said, "If they make it, I want it." Then we spend the second half of life getting rid of the stuff we have accumulated in the first half.

The Bible exhorts us to "not store up... treasures on earth, where moth and rust consume..." (Matthew 6:19). But I have learned ways to protect my stuff against moth and rust. So, I have things that have been a part of my life since my beginning, things that belonged to my mother and father, and toys I played with as a child. Vivian and I spent many hours dragging our two helpless children to auctions and garage sales in search of bargains. And, as I tell people, I may need this stuff some day.

Some of the stuff puts flesh and bone on my memories. I look at this thing or hold that thing and it brings the past to the present; it carries memories from there to here. It may serve no useful purpose today, but like Eeyore's tail in Winnie the Pooh, I have grown sort of attached to it. Sentiment is one of my strong suits.

There are those rare moments when I begin to think straight, when I confess there will come a day when all the stuff will be taken away. Or, to be more accurate, I will be taken away from my stuff. My stuff will remain but I will be put in the ground, "earth to earth, ashes to ashes, dust to dust." I will be finished with the stuff, and it will count for nothing.

So, when we are done with this life, what will count for something?

When I think about those who have left this earth, I
remember words that were spoken, jokes that were told,
kindnesses shown. I remember what was important to them,
what they valued, what they stood for, and what they stood
against. I remember the funny times and the sad times, the times
of achievement and the times of loss. I remember their faith and
their struggles. I remember the moments we spent together, the
memories we created.

That counts.

~

20. Thinking About the Super Bowl, and Stan

I watched the Super Bowl with some friends, and it was one of the few times when the game was as good as the food. David beat Goliath. What is this desire to witness the fall of the mighty? Maybe it's because most of us will never be mighty. Maybe it's because we are envious of the rich, powerful and perfect. We are glad when the ones who always win experience what we have come to know as real life.

Most of us will not win the big game, have our 15 minutes of fame, see our name in lights, or have the world notice when we leave.

Like Stan...

Stan was married to my mom's younger sister, Marian. They lived in Washington State, near a lake, in a house that he built, surrounded by tall evergreen trees. He had been out looking for his dog, came in, sat down in his chair, told Marian he was tired, went to sleep, and never woke up.

He died too soon. But then, to my way of thinking, it is always too soon when someone you love leaves. Stan was an ordinary guy who lived out his life doing ordinary things. He didn't know fame, fortune, or headlines. He would never be considered powerful or mighty. But I believe he was at peace with himself, and with the world around him.

There is a short passage in a letter written by the Christian missionary Paul to a congregation that he helped start in the city of Thessalonica in Macedonia, in which he implores:

And we urge you, beloved, to admonish the idlers, encourage the faint hearted, help the weak, be patient with all of them. See that none of you repays evil for evil, but always seek to do good to one another and to all. Rejoice always, pray without ceasing, give thanks in all circumstances; for this is the will of God in Christ Jesus for you.

1 Thessalonians 5:14-18

That's how Stan lived. He was an unashamed Christian, a follower of Jesus. He was the kind of Christian who gives Christianity a good name. He sought to do good to all, while giving thanks to God.

When I was in high school, my pastor, while leading a Bible study, got on top of a table, took the hand of one of the adults present, and said, "Now I will try to pull you up and you try to pull me down." Well, you know what happened. My pastor said Jesus calls us to do the harder of the two.

The Super Bowl is fun to watch, but it is not real life. Real life is not about winning and losing, nor is it about wanting someone to fail in order for someone else to succeed. It is not about being powerful or perfect, or number one.

Real life is about encouraging others who are having a difficult time. It is about helping those who have no power to help themselves, no advocate to make their voice heard. Real life is about being patient when others become anxious. It is about working to stop the cycle of retribution and revenge that has become the acceptable norm in society. Real life is striving to do good, even when it is hard to lift another up. It is about being glad for faith, thankful for every blessing, and trusting that God will hear your voice at any time. That is perhaps not as exciting as a football game, but I will remember Stan long after I have forgotten who played in the last Super Bowl.

~

21. Jerusalem

Jesus 'set his face to go to Jerusalem' (Luke 9:51). His teaching, healing, and forgiving were not enough. He needed to reach our hearts, so he went to Jerusalem. Christmas makes us feel good. Good Friday breaks our hearts. We need our hearts broken, our very souls invaded. We look at the cross and see the truth about us, who we are. We look again at the cross and see how much God loves us.

In a Peanuts© comic strip by Charles M. Schulz, Linus says to Lucy, "The world does not revolve around you!"

Lucy responds: "You're kidding!"

The other evening, on TV, there was a large orchestra and chorus performing. I marveled at the number of individuals it took to make such beautiful music. Not one of them was named. Not one was front and center. There seemed to be such unselfishness about it all.

Linus tells me the truth about me. That orchestra and chorus give me hope.

It is not true that every day, in every way, we are getting better and better. We will not be fixed to run perfectly, but God can still use us, broken one-note instruments that we are. We need God, to be sure, but we also need one another. In those moments when we reach out, in those moments when we realize we are not the center of the universe and it is possible to be like Christ—forgiving and giving, healing and lifting up another human being in a grace that is unselfish and bold—there is some hope in this very messy, bloody world.

~

22. Preachers

Too often when I listen to preachers, I have the sense that they know a lot about God but very little about me. They quote the Scriptures, explain faith, church, the meaning of the cross, and Easter. But it all seems far removed from what is going on in my life.

There is nothing wrong with what is being said. These are good people, educated and trained in theology, but either they have not lived, or if they have, they refuse to talk about it. Good preaching comes as a result of having lost someone dear or having failed at something. It comes from having discovered one's mortality or from being found out. Good preaching, Gospel preaching, comes out of the realization that life is both messy and precious, that we do terrible things to one another and forgiveness is not only necessary, but possible.

The listener has to be able to say to the preacher, "You understand me, you know me." Otherwise, the preacher is just putting in her time, giving a lecture on God.

~

23. The Fight

I still remember the fight at R.A. Long High School in Longview, Washington. We were in a circle with two boys in the center. There were no rules. One went down and the other kicked him in the face, and there was blood. I don't know why they fought, or who won, or even how it stopped. I do remember the shouting, the voices of those watching, the violence, and the blood.

In chapter 1 of Genesis, we are told that we are created in God's image. God said of all creation, it is very good. In chapter 4 of Genesis, Cain says to his brother, Abel: "Let us go out to the field" (Genesis 4:8). And when they are in the field, Cain rises up against his brother Abel, and kills him.

We were violent almost from our beginning. After Cain kills his brother, there is an exchange between the Lord and Cain, which consists of three questions. God asks: "Where is your brother Abel?" Cain responds, "I do not know." Then he asks: "Am I my brother's keeper?" God does not answer the question, but asks another: "What have you done?" (vv. 9-10)

Then God declares "Listen; your brother's blood is crying out to me from the ground!" (v. 10)

Faith is about questions. We ask God, why? Why is there suffering? Why don't you do something to make things better? God asks us, what have you done to make things better? Why do you keep killing your brother?

According to the Bible there is one God, who created all persons in God's image. It follows that we are connected, related. We are family, dysfunctional for sure, but still family, with a long history of violence.

I have two grandsons, brothers, who have never taken classes in violence, yet hitting and yelling are common, and the word 'mine' is often heard amidst the fray. I suppose it is a small thing and they will learn other ways to disagree and settle disputes, but it is interesting, and sad, that no one needed to teach them to how to fight.

24. It's Deja Vu All Over Again

Those are the words of Yogi Berra, baseball player and manager, commenting on Mickey Mantle and Roger Maris, who repeatedly hit back-to-back home runs in the Yankee seasons of the early 1960s.

My grandfather, Gunder Olson, was born in 1891, in Norway. Here, in his own words, is the story of his coming to this country. He was 19 years old.

I came to the United States on May 3, 1910, with my sister Anna, who was 14 years old. Anna wasn't 15 until August 6. My brother Dagfin borrowed money so I could get here. We came in through Quebec, Canada. We had to have $20 each to get in. Anna had spent hers, so we used mine. She snuck it (the $20 bill) back to me so I had it to show too, before we got off (the boat). Several others borrowed it too, to get off the boat. That money was for food on the train from Quebec to Barton, North Dakota.

It could be argued that my grandfather got into this country illegally, or, at the least, that he broke some rules to get here.

Vivian and I were having a garage sale. A family stopped by to look at our stuff. I could hear the four of them, parents and children, speaking Spanish with one another. As they got ready to leave, the daughter, who looked to be about 10 years old, came to pay for an item.

"May I ask you a question?" I said.

"Yes," she smiled.

"I hear you speaking Spanish with your family. So, do you speak Spanish at home and English at school?" Her smile got bigger; she nodded, and said yes once again.

Grandpa came to this country for economic reasons. He wrote, it was "too hard to make a living in Norway." But it wasn't easy here either.

My mother was born in 1919 and when she was one month old, my grandfather returned to Norway with his wife and three children, because he "was tired of fighting grasshoppers."

53

In 1929 he returned to the United States, leaving his wife and five children in Norway. This time he landed in New York. His sister, Maren, was there to meet him...

I had $10 and Maren was broke, so she got my $10. I had a loaf of bread to eat for the 3-day ride to North Dakota.

A year later, he borrowed money so his family could join him in America. He returned to Norway to visit from time to time, but here is where he lived out his life. He moved from North Dakota to Washington State in 1948. My family (Mom, Dad, me and two sisters) followed Grandpa and Grandma in 1950.

I said to the girl with the wonderful smile, loud enough for her Mom and Dad to hear, "My family came from Norway. When I was about your age, I could speak Norwegian at home and English at school. So we are alike. I hope you will keep speaking Spanish. I have forgotten how to speak Norwegian."

The little girl, who spoke Spanish at home and English in school, thanked me, the old man who once upon a time was a little boy speaking Norwegian at home and English in school. Then she waved good-bye and went after her parents. I watched as her Dad smiled that same beautiful smile, and touched his hand lightly on his daughter's shoulder as they left together.

Jesus says to us, "I was a stranger and you welcomed me." We ask, "And when was it we saw you a stranger and welcomed you?"

Jesus answers, "Truly I tell you, just as you did it to one of the least of these who are members of my family, you did it to me." (Matthew 25)

My grandfather was an immigrant, a stranger in this land. He was one of the least of these. We are a nation of immigrants.

Unless you are Native American, someone in your family came to this country from someplace else – came first, came as a stranger, longing to be welcomed. They still come. And when we welcome the stranger, we welcome Jesus.

25. I Wish For You Christmas

One of the gifts Christmas brings is the gift of memory. We gather with friends and family during the season and tell one another about how we celebrated Christmas "when I was a kid." We talk about the food that was prepared or ask: "Did you open your gifts on Christmas Eve or Christmas Day?" We remember the best toy or the worst gift ever, as if it were last year.

But there are other memories as well. When Vivian and I sit across table from one another to fold our Christmas letter and apply the address labels, we add short notes at the bottom of each typed page. This annual ritual brings to mind our history with these dear people.

We write to Marian and remember it was a year ago that Stan died. We get a letter ready for Darrel and wonder if he might still be staying with his sister after surgery. We write to Marie who will never again celebrate Christmas with her son.

A holiday is fine for the sweet memories of youth, for establishing mealtime traditions, for exchanging presents, or for children playing pageant parts in front of proud parents. But a holiday is not enough for Marian and Darrel and Marie, and maybe not enough for you who must turn your face so that we will not see your tears this season.

Holidays are for going away, for escaping.

Christmas comes.

Christmas looks like a young woman, a girl really, about the age of your average sophomore in high school, whose tiny body is large with child, who clings to her husband as they walk over rough terrain to find a place to be alone.

Christmas smells like a barn that is warm with the odors of straw and animals and manure.

Christmas sounds like mothers crying into the night because of a king who is afraid he will lose his power, so he has all the male children two years and younger killed in the town of Bethlehem.

55

Christmas looks and smells and sounds like real life. We gather with family, exchange gifts, eat and sing and laugh, but Christmas also tells the truth. Life can be hard and harsh. We run to holidays.

Christmas comes.

Christmas comes to Marian. She weeps, but not as one who has no hope. She dares believe that in the Bethlehem child is the promise of eternal life, so her Stan is safe in God's care, even in death. God's promise resides in the same house as her grief, because Christmas comes.

Christmas comes to Darrel, who has endured a year of many surgeries. He trusts his doctors and gives thanks for his faith, a faith that keeps him in good humor, but does not try to fool him. He knows how sick he is, and is comforted that another Christmas comes.

Christmas comes to Marie. The God to whom she prays, whom she addresses as Father, sent his Son to bring us hope and comfort. That Son also died. Such a God can understand her anger and sadness and pain when Christmas comes.

Christmas comes, bringing with it the hope that there is a place prepared for us in heaven above.

Christmas comes, creating in us faith that God is near, as close as a baby's breath.

Christmas comes to hold us when we are no longer able to hold on to God or faith anymore.

Christmas comes, because life is sometimes hard and we get tired.

So in this season, I do not wish for you "happy holidays." I wish for you… Christmas.

~

26. To Find a Sign of Grace
In All the Wrong Places

Today I saw my first sign of spring. Our deck is still covered with a couple of inches of snow, but the door is no longer frozen and there, in the track of the door, belly up to the sun, rests a fairly large black housefly. Some signs of spring are not so pretty.

So it is with grace.

A mother wrote about her son, about finding out that he had a deep neck abscess the size of a tennis ball, which was pressing against an artery leading to the brain. The son had surgery, the abscess was removed, and he recovered fully. It was a terrible ordeal, but in that time of fear and worry, the mother came to a new place of compassion and understanding for all those parents without insurance, without medical facilities, and without a trusted doctor who returns phone calls. That discovery was a grace to her. She learned a new thing—she wants for every child the same care her son received.

That discovery came in the darkest of days, in the midst of a time no parent imagines or deserves. It was not easy, nor desired, but there was a grace found in it all the same.

~

27. Some Words About Marriage
From a Guy Still Learning

The words below were written the year our daughter,
Christin, married Dean. The wedding took place on September
20, 2008, at Joy Ranch near Watertown, South Dakota.

Our daughter is getting married this month. She is not a kid in need of our permission. She is old enough to have completed college, worked for a few years, gone back to school to earn a Masters Degree, and now has the important task of helping people with HIV and AIDS. She has not been dependent upon us for a long time. But she is still our daughter, and her happiness and wellbeing are important to us.

Here we are blessed. For the man she is marrying is a good man, who will pay attention to his wife, who is patient and kind, who will never do her harm. They trust each other and they laugh together.

A person does not need to be married in order to be whole and happy. One is a whole number. You are complete as a single person. I have also said I would rather my daughter be single than married to a jerk. But our daughter is happy and we are happy, and we look forward to this wedding.

At the end of World War II, from his prison cell, Pastor Dietrich Bonhoeffer wrote a wedding sermon for his niece and her future husband.

He tells them it is their love for one another that has brought them to the marriage, and then he writes these words: "It is not love that sustains the marriage, but from now on, the marriage that sustains your love." I think Bonhoeffer is saying that marriage is greater than love, more than emotion or feeling. It is a promise one person makes to the other, a vow that is at the very center of the marriage service. Each one promises to the other: "I will be faithful to you, I will care for you".

According to the Bible, marriage was God's idea. In Genesis 2 we read: "Then the LORD God said: 'It is not good that the man should be alone; I will make him a helper as his partner'... So the LORD God caused a deep sleep to fall upon the man, and he slept; then he took one of his ribs and closed up its place with flesh. And the rib which the LORD God had taken from the man he made into a woman and brought her to the man... Therefore a man leaves his father and his mother and cleaves to his wife, and they become one flesh." (Genesis 2:18, 21, 24)

A woman from Africa was visiting a congregation I served many years ago. She came to tell about the Christian church in her homeland and it was good, serious stuff. Then she caught us off guard when she talked about marriage and asked, with a smile: "Where was woman when God was creating man? She was inside him, close to the man's heart. And where was man when woman was being created? He was asleep, under a tree."

There is no perfect recipe for marriage, but laughter is a necessary ingredient, as is time together and time apart, quiet listening, humility, patience, paying attention, and simply being good to one another.

Mostly it is grace. If the marriage is working, say a prayer of thanks to God, and then say thanks to the one who is sharing this life with you.

~

28. The Importance of Nickels

My wife and I have a joint checking account. I am not good at this so Vivian takes care of it, pays the bills, and keeps us solvent. In June of 2007, I published a little book and decided to keep those expenses and earnings in a different place, so I opened my very own checking account.

I am both careful and slow when it comes to any banking that is my responsibility alone. Each time I make a deposit, I check my numbers against the numbers of the kind women who work behind the counter. Every time they have matched, until the last time. The last time, the bank showed I had five cents more in my account. At first I thought it must be interest earned, so I kept quiet, went home, and checked my account online. I could not find where and why the extra five cents.

The next morning I intended to stop at the bank again, but then I thought they would think I was goofy if I went in to talk about a nickel. Still, that nickel was like a small stone in my shoe.

The importance of nickels goes something like this:

I send a note to a friend. No response from the friend. I send a second note. Still no response… It's no big deal, the note or the response. It's like a nickel. But the absence of a response makes me wonder, is there something broken between us? Foolish, I know. Only a nickel… But it troubles.

A friend retired recently. Rather than sending a card, I wrote a letter. I told him how he had made a difference in my life. I told him how much I appreciated him. I wished him well. It took an hour out my life; a nickel maybe. He cherished the words.

Recently someone told the story of meeting a young man who said I was his pastor and confirmation teacher at one time. The young man said I was the best teacher ever. Well, in truth, I was not a very good teacher. I know that to be a fact, because I was there. But I did strive to pay attention to each and every person in the room.

I wanted every student to know I cared about him or her. Teaching, for me, was difficult; it cost me a lot. But liking the students, paying attention to them, was small change. A nickel.

There is a story in the Bible of two followers of Jesus who are walking from one town to another, sharing their sadness because Jesus is dead and they miss him. A stranger begins to walk with them and they invite him to join them for supper. During the meal this man takes the loaf of bread on the table, breaks it, and shares it with the two friends.

In that ordinary act of breaking bread, they recognize this one who walked with them. It is Jesus himself. They recognize him in this small, simple act of breaking and sharing bread.

The small, simple gestures—the nickels of parents, pastors, teachers, friends—have encouraged and kept me. In those moments of kindness and grace, when they have walked with me and listened to me, Jesus has been revealed. And when I pay attention to the nickel opportunities that come along most every day—the few minutes it takes to listen, to mumble a short prayer, to tell another human being he counts for something—I am convinced that a nickel has great value.

~

29. Four Simple Words

I have this love/hate relationship with the guy who plows our street. I am glad someone comes after a snowfall to do the job. I do love this guy. But then he comes again, after what used to be snow has become something else, something that cannot be formed into a snowball or lifted by the wind, something that no longer makes that sound when your foot pushes through. It is then, when the soft, fluffy stuff has become something else, that this guy, whom I loved the first time he came, comes again, moving ever so quickly (perhaps so I won't recognize him), moving this stuff that used to be snow down the street and leaving a large amount of it in front of my driveway.

In my rational mind, I know this is necessary, but when I encounter this structure resembling the Rocky Mountains at the entrance to my driveway, I am incapable of a rational mind. I do understand, I really do, but after shoveling my driveway six times in five days, to find this fortress blocking the entrance to my very own garage causes my dark side to come forth. God forgive me.

One afternoon, my wife and I left our castle for a trip into the winter wonderland. We did no harm. Ninety minutes later we returned to find that the man and the machine had come. The mountain was there. We both sighed.

Then Vivian saw it. Our mailbox. Our beautiful mailbox with the winter scene was laying in the snow next to the post that once held it. The post itself appeared to be resting at a new angle. Somehow, though grounded in concrete and surrounded by snow and ice, some force was strong enough to tip it.

Many of you worry about old men shoveling snow. As I began moving the mountain, all the while seeing our beloved mailbox resting on its side, I informed my wife I would not have a heart attack because of snow, but there was a possibility my blood pressure was rising for other reasons.

Once the mountain was moved, the car was in the garage, and the mailbox was tied to the post with some thin rope, I called the street department and left a message. The next morning Mike called. I told him what had happened. Mike said four simple words.

"I am very sorry."

I don't know if he learned these words from his mother or his wife or his church, or from his own experience, but he said them. He said them twice in the two minutes we spoke. He didn't have to say them. He wasn't the plow driver who played chicken with my mailbox. But he said them anyway. Bless him for that. I know people who do not say these words, ever. They find an excuse or put the blame on someone else, as they are unable to say: "I am very sorry."

The mailbox is still tied to the post with a rope, the snow will fall, and the guy on the machine will come and leave that strange stuff on my driveway. But those words bring comfort, and are cause for hope.

These are some of the best and most necessary words we say to one another. These four simple words make things better every single time.

~

30. What is Truth?

When Jesus is brought before Pilate for trial, he says to Pilate: "For this I was born and for this I came into the world, to testify to the truth" (John 18:37). Pilate responds: "What is truth?" Jesus does not answer that question, but leaves it hanging in the air.

What is truth? What can we count on? What truth do we hold amidst all the changes in life?

There was a time when it was true that it was impossible for human beings to fly. The truth changed on October 17, 1903, when two brothers named Wright changed the truth.

There was a time when it was true that American women couldn't vote. The truth changed on August 26, 1920, with the 19th Amendment.

We say, in the Church to which I belong (the Evangelical Lutheran Church in America), that women can be pastors. It was not always so. There was a time when we said women cannot be pastors, and we proved it by quoting Bible verses that clearly state that women are to keep silent in the church.

We changed our minds.

We are free to change our minds because God changes. In Exodus 32, God is disappointed with the people of Israel, and says to Moses, "Your people, whom you brought up out of the land of Egypt, have acted perversely" (Exodus 32:7). God goes on to tell Moses that his anger will consume them.

Moses pleads for the people: "God, you acted to free your people from captivity. If you do destroy these people, Egypt will say that God brought them out of Egypt, only to destroy them in the mountains. Remember Abraham, Isaac, and Israel, and remember your promise to them of this great nation."

"And the LORD changed his mind about the disaster that he planned to bring on his people" (v. 14).

If God changes His mind and if the church changes her mind, what do we hang onto?

Jesus says: "If you continue in my word, you are truly my disciples; and you will know the truth and the truth will make you free... So if the Son makes you free, you will be free indeed" (John 8:31-32, 36).

According to Jesus, the truth and the Son are synonymous. Pilate was looking truth in the eye and still did not see.

The question is not, what is truth? Rather, who is the truth? It is not right doctrine that saves. It is not belonging to the right denomination that is the truth. The whole point of the Reformation in the time of Martin Luther was to lead us back to Jesus. "Christ alone, grace alone, faith alone."

When we tie our faith to a Bible verse, to an ideology, to a doctrine, or to a cause, no matter how righteous, we may look truth right in the eye and still not see.

Martin Luther said: "The Bible is the cradle wherein Christ is laid." We do not worship the cradle, nor do we worship the Bible. It's easy to find a verse in scripture that supports what we believe. We hurl Bible verses back and forth like grenades.

The sin to which Jesus says we are slave is not the bad things we do or the good things we fail to do, but a lack of trust in God and in one another. Our sin is the insecurity that Jesus is not quite enough, that we need Jesus plus some other conviction or cause. Our sin is our need to be right and therefore righteous on our own terms, giving witness to our insecurity that we cannot quite trust God and God's righteousness. So we will try to bolster our status and build our own righteousness by making up a list of things we must do or must not do.

We will differ as Christians on a whole bunch of stuff, but none of that stuff is finally the truth. Jesus is the truth and Jesus sets us free to live in relationship with God and with one another. We have been created for such relationships, and we are neither whole nor free apart from those relationships.

Jesus sets us free to disagree with each other and free to hold a variety of opinions on a variety of subjects. Our unity, our oneness, our hope, our salvation, our faith is in him.

Jesus sets us free from the need to justify ourselves on our own terms. He makes it clear that we are all sinners in need of forgiveness. No one is righteous, or right, all of the time. So we rest, all of us, in the love of God, knowing that we need not find cause to justify ourselves, for we are justified already by the grace of God through faith in Jesus, who is our truth.

~

31. Deadwood and Deer
And Living Out Who We Are

Vivian and I were in Deadwood for the South Dakota
Festival of Books. We stayed in a motel at the edge of town and
each morning enjoyed our breakfast in a second floor room.

One morning we glanced out the window and saw two small
deer, delicate and precise, walking across the side of the rocky
hill. There were six other diners in the room. Two men at one
table looked up, but four women at another table did not. I
walked over to them and pointed, inviting them to see the deer.
Two of the women did look, but the other two continued to eat
their bagels and cream cheese and commented that they had seen
deer before.

There was no way anyone could stop me from sharing the
joy of seeing those deer. Pointing out the deer was as much fun
as seeing the deer. I saw something beautiful and good, and
wanted to tell my neighbors.

So we talk about the football game we attended or the movie
we saw or the last trip we took. We talk about our children and
grandchildren. Such sharing is not difficult. No one has to make
us do it; it is something we want to do.

But talking about our faith is a different matter. Most of us
become shy when there is an opportunity to say something about
that which is so much a part of our lives. We worship, we pray,
we give, we work, because of the faith that is in us. Yet to tell
another about what we believe and to talk about God is difficult
for most of us.

But in truth, we do give witness to our faith whether we
intend to or not, whether we even say anything at all.

The resurrected Jesus said to the church: "You will be my
witnesses" (Acts 1:8). The words are spoken not as command,
but as promise. Jesus is saying: "You will give witness of me,
because you are mine and bear my name."

67

How we conduct our affairs gives evidence of what we believe. How we treat others speaks loudly about how God treats us. There is no guarantee anyone will notice or care. They may just go on eating their bagels and cream cheese. Still, there is a joy in being faithful to who we are. It feels good to conduct our lives as children of God.

Martin Luther even dared to suggest that we, who are followers of Jesus, are little Christs in the world. We give witness of God's love, not so that we may become children of God, but because we already are children of God.

And maybe some day, at some time, we may even say something about it.

32. Garage Sale at the Cemetery

A simple sign is posted
at the corner of the cemetery.
GARAGE SALE!
What could be for sale
at a cemetery?
What would one not want
or need anymore?
Regrets? Failures?
Who would buy such?
Won't sell at any price.
But do you have some laughter
left over or some sweet
conversation you
no longer need?
Of course you will
hang unto the memories,
and the dreams, even
those unfulfilled.

33. Writing the Last Chapter

I have three sisters. We try to get together once a year. The four of us are old, or pretty darn close to old, so when we gather we find ourselves talking about where we hurt and how well we sleep, how many pills we take, and how expensive everything has become. All indications that we are old.

The four of us were talking about the generation just above us, the generation of our parents. We noted that on our Dad's side, all had left this earth. On Mom's side, of the six brothers and sisters, one brother and two sisters live. Merna remarked that it must be hard to see all your siblings die, and she continued: "I sure wouldn't want to be the last to go."

Then there was a very long pause...

"But I don't want to be the first either."

We also talk about change. When one achieves a certain age, having experienced a multitude of changes over the years, one comes to realize that change will not destroy the universe, or life as we know it. We are not like the young who meet change with joy and expectation; we come out to meet it at a slower pace. But we will not be afraid. Change has no real power over us, unless we want to believe it so. Change is something outside; it cannot shape who we are inside, and it cannot destroy what we believe and who we are as children of God.

Change seems to have more power to frighten us in our middle years, perhaps because then we are beginning to learn the truth; we may not be in charge. Not only are we not in charge of the world around us, we are not even in charge of our own lives. We become acquainted with our mortality. When we are older, when we have lived with that truth for a time, death loses its power to frighten us.

Death is not so much about being afraid of what lies ahead as it is about missing what gets left behind.

What a wonderful world this is and how brief our time here. Maybe we do learn some things as we begin the last chapter. Maybe we do learn how good it is to make time to be with our children, to go for a walk with our spouse, or to tell our friends how much we appreciate them.

~

34. Going to Church

It's an old joke. A guy is golfing, having a terrible game. His caddy is following behind. After a particularly disastrous hole, the golfer says quietly to the caddy: "Golf is a funny game, isn't it?"

"Yes," the caddy replies, "but it's not supposed to be."

Perhaps the same could be said about worship or 'going to church.' It's a funny game.

I have been attending or leading worship for a long time, but still cannot explain it. Sometimes it is funny, in that funny things happen. Sometimes it is just plain foolishness as we fight over furniture and songs. I have claimed I could preach heresy and no one would notice, but I had better be prepared for battle if I dare suggest new carpet.

Once in a while, something glorious happens, a holy moment. There is a silence that enables one to hear God. There is a word spoken that reveals a grace. There is the taste of wine that quenches a thirst that is not physical. There is a presence, unseen and unheard, that is as real as anything can be. Sometimes faith is born. Sometimes hope is renewed. Sometimes forgiveness is known.

Though it cannot always be explained, at times worship brings a mercy that breaks the heart and we are glad for it, even when we do not understand it. Worship can be glorious and beautiful, yet as messy and ordinary as real life.

Worship is for people who have done shameful deeds during the past week, and it is for those who would not get caught dead sharing space with people who do shameful things. Together we come before God, which is the way it should be.

We may 'go to church' for all the wrong reasons, but that is rather beside the point. What's important is that we do come together, and we may hear the word of God, and we may decide it a good time to speak to God. The coming together has that kind of potential.

In a nation of people often convinced that we are gods, it is marvelous that there are some who question this assumption and say so aloud. In a time when there are people ready to beat up anyone who suggests we remove 'under God' from a pledge (as if such a beating would meet with the approval of Jesus), it is good to gather with a foolish few who actually attempt to live 'under God' and not simply mouth the words in a pledge.

We worship not because we are moral people, but because we are mortal people who have reason to be ashamed of our behavior and dare to believe there is a God and God still cares.

~

35. Something Happened

When the sabbath was over, Mary Magdalene and Mary the mother of James and Salome brought spices, so that they might go and anoint him. And very early on that first day of the week, when the sun had risen, they went to the tomb... They saw a young man, dressed in a white robe, sitting on the right side; and they were alarmed. But he said to them: "Do not be alarmed. You are looking for Jesus of Nazareth, who was crucified. He has been raised; he is not here. But go, tell..." So they went out and fled from the tomb, for terror and amazement had seized them; and they said nothing to anyone, for they were afraid."
Mark 16:1-8

Something happened. Of that, there can be no doubt, because it changed everything. After that day, nothing was the same for those who had once walked the dusty roads with him and heard his stories and watched his compassion. They who knew him, who knew of his death... nothing was the same for them after that single Sunday morning.

At first it was only the terror of it – the unspeakable terror. Even though they were assured, "Do not be afraid. Do not be alarmed." Even though they were asked only to "Go tell." Still they said nothing to anyone, because they were afraid.

There was nothing glorious about it. No magnificent sunrise; no angel choir; no booming voice from heaven. There were only the faithful women who refuse to forget, who go to the cemetery to honor and to weep. Then the empty tomb and someone – a stranger, a young man, a messenger – saying simply: "He has been raised. Go tell."

And the terror.

When the terrified women do finally tell, it seems to those who hear it, 'an idle tale.'

That is how it begins in the early morning quiet.

And at times, were we to tell the truth, it still seems an idle tale. And we are still afraid. But something did happen; that we cannot deny. For they who had walked with him, touched his hand, heard his voice, were changed, and finally they did tell. Perhaps still afraid, but they did tell.

The telling has come down through the years, from parent to child, from friend to neighbor, from stranger to stranger, from child to parent, and we who have heard the telling have believed, even in the midst of our unbelief and our fear... and we tell.

In our coming together to worship, we tell. With our lives, striving to follow his path and do his will, we tell. With our words, speaking hope, and with our silence too, listening with compassion, we tell.

We tell what we have seen and heard and felt and dare believe.

We tell that the last enemy, death, has been destroyed because he has been raised.

Something happened. Of that, there can be no doubt.

~

36. A Thing of Beauty is a Joy Forever

I am in Stillwater, Minnesota on a warm day in May, in a theological bookstore that's located in a building that was once a church. I am searching through row upon row of books, when I hear the sound of someone coming in through the door just off to my left. I glance up. She looks to be about thirty years old,

John Keats by William Hilton

dressed from the top of her head to the top of her shoes in white. I am sure she is a Catholic sister, and I am sure she is beautiful. She greets me with a smile and a nod of her head, and as I return the greeting, she moves past me further into the store. A short time later I sense movement to my right, and look up to see her again as she is leaving.

As she passes, she once again greets me with a smile and a nod of her head. Again I return the greeting. Then, as she is about to go out the door, I say to her back: "By the way, you look quite beautiful, you know."

She turns, blushes, smiles, and says, "Thank you." Then as she goes out the door, she adds, perhaps to herself, perhaps to God, "I love wearing this habit."

I have no lesson here. I simply like that young Catholic sister in her white habit. I like her smile, the blush on her cheeks, the fact that she likes wearing her habit and likes looking beautiful in it. I cherish those few moments in her presence and doubt I will ever forget them.

Often beauty will come, unexpected and undeserved, like a gentle rain in the midst of a dry summer. Our only work is to take notice and give thanks. Still again, we make choices in life. We can choose to look for beauty, goodness, and grace, or we can close our eyes, stop our ears, and howl like some wounded creature caught in a trap, damning all, refusing all, and loving nothing. We can be so inwardly turned as to find no joy in another's joy, no compassion for another's plight, and no desire to reach out and lift up someone who has fallen. Or we can recognize our own need to be loved and figure out that perhaps such is also true for everyone else in this world.

We can search out beauty, and when it is found, we can cherish the finding, give thanks to God for such a blessing as this, and hold it in our heart for all time. As John Keats (1795-1821) tells us in his epic poem Endymion: "A thing of beauty is a joy forever."

~

37. Pure Love

When I was a child, I spoke like a child, I thought like a child, I reasoned like a child.

1 Corinthians 13:11

Vivian and I have two grandsons, Benjamin Magnus and Samuel Finn (the Mighty Finn).

When the Mighty Finn was three years old, he would walk around the house with no shoes or socks on and tell his dad he was barefoot because "bears don't wear shoes."

When Finn was four years old, sitting next to his aunt (our daughter Christin), he turned to her and asked, for no obvious reason, "Are you out of your mind?"

As Christin was leaving one day, Finn shouted after her, "Goodbye, stupid." His grandmother stopped him with her best grandmotherly look and voice, and said: "Finn, we don't call people stupid." Without skipping a beat, Finn turned back to Christin, waved, and said: "Goodbye, my love."

When the boys were about seven and five, Grandma and Finn were playing a game on the floor. Benjamin, who was nearby, put his hand on the top of a toy truck and gave it a push. I looked up from my reading. Benjamin soon realized that if he pushed down on the truck as he simultaneously pushed it in a circle, it would squeak. So he pushed the truck and the truck went in a circle, squeaking all the way.

Squeak, squeak, squeak.

I noticed that all the while Benjamin was pushing the truck, he was also keeping an eye on his younger brother. And there was a tiny smile on his face. It was truly an irritating sound, this squeak, squeak, squeak, but I endured it. I wondered how the other two people in the room were doing. I soon found out when Finn jumped up from the floor, raised his two arms in the air and shouted: "He's driving me crazy!"

78

Their Mom and Dad left the boys at our house for a few days. We were playing a card game where the object is to collect as many cards as possible. I was losing. Finn looked at me and said, "Grandpa, you are the baddest player here." I hung my head and mumbled something about feeling bad. Finn said: "Grandpa, I don't mean to make you feel bad, but just look at your cards."

During the week of his seventh birthday, Finn was walking home from school with his grandmother. They took their time, picked up some leaves and looked at some bugs. As they slowly strolled home, Finn said, "Grandma, we are making memories."

That same week, Finn was busy playing at something. His grandmother started to talk to him. Without turning away from his play, he said: "I'm busy right now. I will get back to you later. At the sound of the beep, please leave a message. BEEP!"

I will tell you what pure love looks like. Pure love is about twenty-nine inches tall, with yellow silk at the top and ten toes at the bottom, proud of his belly button and an expert at smiling. He will walk on those toes for no reason except that he can. When he sees me from the across the room he runs, arms outstretched, fingers moving with excitement, almost falling down in his joy, motor squealing – up, up he comes and burrows into my neck, like some creature finding his home. I am that home and this is pure love.

~

38. A Standing Ovation

Our high school youth group had been invited by the chaplain at the state hospital to lead a Sunday evening worship service in the chapel. We had done this before and looked forward to our journey.

We had discovered during our previous visits that the responses by the congregation in this particular setting were often a surprise. On Sunday morning, in most congregations, there is a kind of routine, an established agenda: this is when you stand, this is when you sit, this is when you sing, this is when you listen, etc. We were prepared, from our previous visits, for members of this congregation to stand when they felt like it, to leave at any moment, to ask a question, or to come forward and shake hands with the person who was reading.

But this time something new happened. When a young high school student finished reading the Gospel, the congregation... clapped.

They heard the good news of God's love, and they applauded.

~

39. To Live So Connected to the Land

I have often said that my father's body moved to Washington State, but his heart remained in North Dakota. The barn had burned to the ground. That loss seemed to be connected to our leaving, but I was too young to comprehend all the fine points of our lives. I remember the auction—a bed was sold for twenty-five cents. The house was left empty, not sold or taken down, but simply vacated as if there were an intention to return.

Dad received the Rugby newspaper until he died. He kept up with families and the price of wheat and barley. For the rest of his life he complained about the high cost of machinery, seed, fertilizer, and the low return for the crops harvested.

What is it about the land? Is it that we come from the earth? The book of Genesis testifies: "The LORD God formed man from the dust of the ground." (Genesis 2:7) Later God tells Adam: "You shall return to the ground, for out of it you were taken; you are dust, and to dust you shall return." (Genesis 3:19)

What I believe I have discovered over the years is that there are no 'country bumpkins' who farm the land. Farm people are bright, hard working, and fiercely independent.

It is a way of living one's life. It is about the earth and the seasons, about sunshine and rain, about participating in birth and death, about creation and life, about faith and planting and miracle, about being independent while being dependent, and understanding that both can be true and good.

You can wash the dirt out from under a farmer's fingernails, but you can never get it out of his soul.

40. Oscar Winners Live Longer

In 2001 there was a study published in *Annals of Internal Medicine* on the effects that winning the Academy Award have on an actor's self-esteem. The study, done by Dr. Donald A. Redelmeier and Sheldon Singh, found that Oscar winners live nearly four years longer than either actors who were never nominated or those who were nominated and did not win. Multiple winners are even more fortunate, living an average of six years longer than their colleagues. The authors say that the results cannot be explained away by higher income, because even actors who do not win tend to be wealthy and so can afford good health care.

Another scholar, Theodore Marmor, co-editor of the book *Why Are Some People Healthy and Others Not,* said people who win Oscars feel as if they have taken care of "one of the great sources of anxiety in the world of entertainment: will anybody notice?"

When Sally Field won an Oscar for the second time, she responded: "The first time I didn't feel it, (but now) I can't deny the fact that you like me! Right now, you really like me!"

How fragile we are, how much love we all need.

When I was teaching confirmation classes, young girls would come into class crying because someone had said something hurtful. Later I would witness that same child hurling hurtful words at another classmate. For some odd reason, it did not connect that the person she was harming might feel as she had felt just an hour earlier.

It would seem our need to be liked, to be understood, to be loved, does not always translate into our care and understanding of the other person.

~

41. Finding Something to Wear

Once upon a time, while visiting our son and his family, we went to an outdoor swimming pool. This was something I had not done for a long time. It was a hot day and the pool was filled with people. While watching my family (including the two grandsons) and a whole bunch of strangers getting in and out of the water – splashing, diving, walking around the pool and having a great time – I came to realize how much I appreciate clothes.

Dogs, cats, horses, even cows, look just fine with no clothes on. In fact, put clothes on any of them and they look downright silly. But it seems to me that human beings are meant to wear clothes in public.

One gentleman, who appeared to be about forty years old and is perhaps a fine human being, was wearing a tiny piece of cloth that, according to my daughter-in-law, is called a Speedo®. It looked to be at least a couple of sizes too small and apparently he never intended to use it for swimming, as he kept parading around, never once getting wet.

For human beings, clothing is a great idea.

The apostle Paul wrote to the congregation at Colossae: "As God's chosen ones, holy and beloved, clothe yourselves with compassion, kindness, humility, meekness, and patience." (Colossians 3:12)

I hear people say they still like Jesus, but have given up on the church. Perhaps in part because we have forgotten what to wear.

"Above all, clothe yourselves with love, which binds everything together in perfect harmony." (Colossians 3:14)

Never goes out of style.

If you are a follower of Jesus, you are the church. Wherever you might find yourself, you are the church. Whoever you are with, you are the church. Whatever activities you participate in, you are the church.

You are the church: forgiving sin, healing the sick and raising the dead. Freya Stark (1893-1993) said: "There can be no happiness if the things we believe in are different from the things we do."

You are a living, breathing invitation to faith in God.

~

42. A Letter from Martin Luther

In a letter to Philip Melanchthon in August of 1521, Martin Luther wrote: "Be a sinner and sin boldly, but believe and rejoice in Christ even more boldly. For he is victorious over sin, death, and the world. As long as we are here we have to sin. This life is not the dwelling place of righteousness but, as Peter says, we look for a new heaven and a new earth in which righteousness dwells. Pray boldly—you too are a mighty sinner."*

Luther strips away all our self-righteousness, all our judgment upon others, and all the excuses we make for our bad behavior. He reminds us to acknowledge our wrongdoing, make confession of our sin boldly and honestly, without fear. Do not fear that God will turn aside from you, but fear that you will miss God's voice of judgment and mercy, and fail to hear the invitation to go work in God's kingdom.

We are meant to create, to accomplish, to work as God worked, and to rest as God rested, for we are God's children made in God's image. When we work, when we act, and when we create, we will often get it wrong. We will fail, we will sin; of this there is no doubt. So go ahead: work, create, accomplish without fear. Do something, knowing that even as you fail, even when you do not accomplish that which is good and right and pure, God still holds you as a loving parent holds a child.

When you finally go back to dust, know that you did something—that you did your very best—all the while trusting in the deep, deep love of God.

~

*Luther to Melanchthon, letter no. 99, August 1, 1521, from Dr. Martin Luther's Saemmtliche Schriften, translated by Erika Bullmann Flores, Concordia Publishing House, N. D., Vol. 15, cols 2585-2590.

43. The Difference Between Men and Women

In the midst of a service of worship,
while the sermon was being preached,
there came the cry of an upset child,
then sound of feet
moving quickly up the aisle.

Children have pleaded for help
on many a Sunday morning,
so this was ordinary, common stuff.
But I noticed something new,
perhaps evidence of a truth in us.

At the sound of this child,
every female in the room turned around.
I presume to see if help was needed.
Yet every male stared straight ahead.
The women volunteered while the men retreated.

44. They Got Up

As Jesus was walking along, he saw a man called Matthew sitting at the tax booth; and he said to him, "Follow me." And he got up and followed him.

Matthew 9:9

While he was saying these things to them, suddenly a leader of the synagogue came in and knelt before him, saying, "My daughter has just died; but come and lay your hand on her, and she will live." And Jesus got up and followed him.

Matthew 9:18-19

Matthew is sitting at the tax booth; Jesus comes by and invites him to follow. Matthew gets up and follows Jesus.

A short time later, a man from the synagogue comes to Jesus, kneels before him, and pleads with him to come because his daughter has just died. Jesus gets up and follows the father.

Matthew and Jesus both 'get up' and follow.

My friend who has Parkinson's once said to me: "When I am sitting down and I wish to get up, I have to say to my legs, 'get up now'. It will take some time and it will not be automatic or easy, but I keep telling my legs, 'get up,' and finally they get up, and the rest of me follows." Each time of getting up for my friend is a deliberate decision, a matter of the heart and the mind and the body.

We are invited to get up and follow Jesus, who gets up and follows after the poor and the hungry, after those whose hearts are wounded, whose spirits are broken, and those filled with guilt and shame, longing for mercy and justice and some peace in their lives.

Getting up is a brave thing, for you may not know how it will go and what you will find, or if anyone will go with you. But it is a grace.

When you get up and follow after someone who needs help, and you get there, you will find Jesus. You can tell by the way your heart feels.

We are told in the gospel of Luke, chapter 24, that on that first Easter morning some women go to the tomb to anoint the dead body of Jesus. They find the tomb empty and are confronted by two men who tell the women that Jesus "is not here, but has risen."

The women find the disciples and tell them what happened to them. Then we read this response of the church: "But these words seemed to them an idle tale, and they did not believe them."

The church, including Peter, did not believe the words of the women.

But Peter got up.

"…Peter got up and ran to the tomb; stooping and looking in, he saw the linen clothes by themselves; then he went home, amazed at what had happened." Luke 24:13

It seemed an idle tale, but he got up anyway.

In the midst of his unbelief, in the middle of his sneaking suspicion that the women are a bit delirious, goofy in the head, caught up in wishful thinking, Peter got up. In spite of all past evidence to the contrary, evidence that dead is dead, Peter go up. The result is amazement.

Still no proof…

Still no body, dead or alive…

But the tomb is empty and Peter is amazed. And it came to be so, because he got up.

The other option is to sit there.

~

45. Therefore

I rode the bus to school. It was a part of my life from grade school through my senior year in high school. I left our house, walked up the gravel driveway, turned left, then traveled a short distance on paved road to the bus stop. There I stood with a small group of friends and enemies, depending upon morning moods and the ages of those assembled, and waited for the school bus.

My Mom insisted I wear a cap. No one wore a cap.

So each morning I put the cap on my head, walked up the driveway, removed the cap, stuck it in my back pocket, and turned left, beyond my mom's vision. In the afternoon I got off the bus, went to the top of the gravel, put the cap on my head, and walked down the driveway home. I followed that routine for years.

In a conversation with my mom after graduation, I made confession of my sin. She then made absolution by telling me that she was well aware of my pretense, almost from the beginning.

Her job was to do her best for me, to place a cap upon my head for protection from hot sun and cold rain. If I refused, she would not bend me to her will.

Her rule, as all good rules, was for my sake, not for her sake. Or for the sake of the rule…

She knew what was good for me. Her law was a gift. I refused the gift.

The law is good. But forgiveness and life are not found in the law or in rules. There was one who placed a cap on my head each morning, watched as I stuck the cap in my back pocket, smiled at my pride, and welcomed me home with open arms. She was saying, I am the one who gave you life, who would give up life for you, who loves you with an everlasting love, therefore…

The 'therefore' comes out of love.

46. A Small Good Thing

I read in the paper that a mother had died. I knew her son.
He was not so young and she was old enough so the
announcement of her death was not shocking, but he was still a
son whose Mom has died. The paper said the visitation was that
afternoon. I put on some nicer clothes and drove to the funeral
home. The son saw me come into the room; he smiled and
thanked me for coming. We visited. I met his siblings. We talked
about his Mom. We laughed. I left after a few minutes. It was a
small thing, so fleeting, so easy for me to do. But it was, I
believe, a good thing. The son was blessed, as were his brother
and sisters, I believe. I know for certain I was blessed. It felt
good to tell someone that I remembered and liked his mother,
and was sad for her leaving. It was good to see this son, to see
his smile, hear his voice, and touch his hand once again.

~

47. This Cup

used to be on my desk
but then we moved
and I put it in a box
which I found and
then remembered
why I kept
this beautiful cup
with the missing handle
which I found long ago
and kept though broken
because it reminds me
that a cup can be useful
and beautiful
even though broken
and people
are the same way

48. Agree to Disagree

When we lived in Gayville, in southeast South Dakota, our neighbors Swede and Ardys were members of our congregation and good friends. I watched as Ardys was mowing the lawn one day. As the clouds gathered, I saw her look up, saw that she was not close to being done with the mowing, saw a few drops of rain come down, and finally saw Ardys raise her fist to the sky and shake it.

It rained.

Sometimes when you want the sun to shine, it rains. Sometimes the good suffer. Sometimes bad things happen to good people. Sometimes, it is as if God is not paying attention. Sometimes you want to shake your fist at the heavens and curse God.

And sometimes you keep mowing even when it is raining. Ardys did.

49. I Will Tell You a Story

A pastor friend in Brookings asked if I would come to his church and help him one weekend. He serves a large congregation and the other pastor had not been able to work because of health problems. My friend asked if I could preach on Saturday evening and again Sunday morning, thereby giving him time away from preparation for one week; time he could devote to other work.

It is a fifty-mile drive to Brookings, and I would be making the round trip journey twice that weekend. My car has one of those gadgets that tells you how many more miles you can drive with the amount of fuel in the gas tank. I calculated I could make the round trip on Saturday and get to Brookings the next morning, but would need to put gas in the car before driving home after worship on Sunday.

All went well. The time with my pastor friend and his congregation was good. I had a safe trip there and back home on Saturday, and a quiet drive the next morning. After worship on Sunday I said goodbye to Pastor Herb, and headed home. Perfect.

About twenty miles from Watertown, there appeared a tiny light, a light I had never noticed before. Then and only then did I remember. I reached up, pushed the little button above my head and the fancy gadget told me what I feared. I was twenty miles from home and I had enough gas to drive thirteen miles.

It is difficult to panic while driving alone. There is no room to jump around, no bed to lie down upon and cry, no wall to beat one's head against, and no one to hear you scream. All the panic takes place in your head, all the screaming is silent, and there is no one to share this most helpless feeling, and later no one to walk with you to the nearest gas station.

What does happen though, in times such as this, is that one's faith grows and prayer takes on a new energy.

This is not the quiet sober prayer of one who is concerned but not really anxious about life, or the controlled, prepared prayer of a preacher on Sunday, a prayer that is sometimes more like an announcement for the people in the pew. ("God bless Alma Lu who had surgery last Tuesday in Sioux Falls and who is now recovering at home, but hopes to be back to work next week. Amen.") This is something quite different. This is honest, urgent, and pretty simple. Basically, one cries, "Help!"

Now, I do not believe prayer is magic. If one jumps off a high building and prays that he will not hit the ground, chances are he will hit the ground. If the gas tank in my car is empty, my prayer will not fill it, otherwise why bother to stop at gas stations. I do pray for the sick, but I also encourage the sick to get to a doctor.

I believe prayer does not so much change the situation as it changes the one who prays. If I pray that something be done about hunger in the world, then I had better do something to help elevate hunger where and when I can. My prayer might be, "God give me the wisdom to know what to do and the willingness to get off my backside."

C. S. Lewis taught me that one of the powerful and refreshing things we can learn from the prayers in the Book of Psalms is honesty. Psalm 10 begins, "God, are you avoiding me? Where are you when I need you?"[*]

There is no need to pretty up our prayers. Like good conversation, prayer is best when it is honest.

God knows what we need, but we still pray because the one we follow, Jesus, has asked us to pray. I think Jesus does so because he cares about us and knows the blessing prayer brings to the one who prays. The Twelve who followed Jesus at the beginning must have watched him pray, must have seen it was a good thing, because they said to him, "Lord, teach us to pray." (Luke 11:1) Jesus told them to talk to God like a child to a loving parent, asking for ordinary things like food and forgiveness and help along the way.

There is a mystery about prayer, for sure, and it would be false on my part to say that I understand anything at all about this gift, but we are better for it. It can change us and it can keep us.

Shortly after discovering I had enough gas to travel thirteen miles, I saw a sign naming two towns. I turned off the highway. The town to the east was ten miles away and the town to the west was nine miles away. I pushed the button and learned I had enough gas for nine miles. I headed west.

The temptation I now faced was to drive as fast as possible. But I also knew that by driving faster I was using up the gas faster, so I tried to control this desire. When I got to the edge of town, the gadget said one mile. I had no idea where a gas station was located. I took the first turn south. I later discovered that a bit further west there was a station on the north edge of town, but I didn't know that when I turned south. I drove almost to the south edge of town, looked right and there was a gas station two or three blocks away. I turned right, got behind a very slow driver who, thankfully, could not hear what I was saying about his driving, and moved ever so (painfully) slowly toward my goal, an old gas station that had adapted new technology and took credit cards. Praise God.

When I arrived, I did three things: I looked at the gadget which still read one mile, filled my car with gas, and said a prayer of thanks. Not necessarily in that order.

~

50. Anxious for Christmas

It was November 15. I was driving in town, slowed down to make a right turn and saw a pickup truck parked in a driveway. In the bed of the truck there was a Christmas tree. My first thought was, here is a family anxious for Christmas.

I know some people grumble about stores selling ornaments and cards too early, lights on houses, and trees decorated in November. To some it seems wrong. They say: "We used to wait until after Thanksgiving, but no more. We can't wait."

The children can't wait because they know there will be presents. I remember how anxious I was. Even though there would not be many gifts, I knew there would be something special for me under the tree. I still have the cap gun with the white belt and holster and the bow with the quiver for the arrows. I remember the extended family gatherings in our small home for the traditional Norwegian meal of lutefisk and boiled potatoes with lots of melted butter. I certainly remember the women saying: "We will not open any presents until we eat our dinner and the dishes are all put away."

For sure, we children were anxious, saying, "Hurry up! Hurry up!"

But it is more than receiving gifts. We are anxious for Christmas because we like what it does to us. We give to others, write letters, gather with family and friends. We put money in a kettle to help people we don't know. We greet each other and we make sure that those who are struggling to make ends meet have food on the table and toys for the kids. We even go to church in the middle of the week. We visit people in nursing homes. We, who can't sing, sing anyway. All because it is Christmas...

No, it's never too early for Christmas.

Once again we reach out our arms to hold this baby near our hearts. We smile and relax just a bit, filled with the wonder of this life, so pure, so gentle. This child cannot help but change us for the better.

On that first Christmas night, the angel said to the shepherds: "Do not be afraid." (Luke 2:10) What is there to fear from a baby? A baby is powerless, with no guile, no anger, and no judgment, only needing from us without fearing we will not provide: simply trusting, and content to be resting in our arms. This is how God came. This is Christmas. This one child, and for a time, perhaps too brief, our fears are taken over by our love for this child and he is able to change our hearts.

"This will be a sign for you," the angel said to the shepherds. "You will find a child wrapped in bands of cloth and lying in a manger." (v. 12) At each Christmas we, too, find our way to this baby and are glad. The apostle Paul wrote to the congregation in the town of Colossae: "Jesus is the image of the invisible God… For in him the fullness of God was pleased to dwell." (Colossians 1:15, 19)

We will light the lights, decorate the tree, buy the gifts, send the cards, gather with family, and greet one another. All of this is good, but we know deep within ourselves that all of it is only the wrapping. We know the gift is the baby, this one particular child named Jesus.

"You are to name him Jesus," said the angel to Joseph, "for he will save his people from their sins." (Matthew 1:21)

In Jesus, we are free to live life as fully and as joyfully as we will allow ourselves. For it is only we who hold ourselves back. God does not. For God has forgiven us in this baby and will not restrain us from living with sheer abandon, trusting in this gentle and gracious God, who keeps telling us: "Do not be afraid."

When Christmas comes each year, we catch a glimpse of who we are meant to be in our giving, in our joy, and in our care for those with little power in this world.

We are better people at Christmas.

Of course we are anxious for Christmas.

~

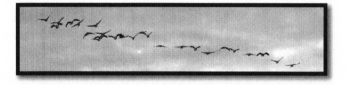

A Morning Word

Husbands, love your wives,
as Christ loved the church…
Children… honor your father and mother…
Fathers, do not provoke your children
to anger…

Ephesians 5:25; 6:1, 4

A Morning Prayer

Gracious God, I give you thanks
this day for the blessing of family.
I thank you for those who know me,
inside and out, who love me,
care for me, forgive me, pray for me,
and will weep when I leave this earth.
Grant me wisdom and kindness
as I live with my family.
Amen.

51. It All Began With Aspen

I will share more detail than perhaps you will consider necessary, but I believe the details are important in the telling of this story, so please bear with me.

I am a pastor in the Evangelical Lutheran Church in America. The ELCA has a website called ELCA Good Gifts (community.elca.org). There, one can purchase "gifts that make a difference," gifts to help people, gifts to save lives. Every forty-five seconds a child dies of malaria. At ELCA Good Gifts you can buy malaria net that may save a life. Or you can buy a blanket or a goat or a pig or even ten chicks to bring hope and real help to people.

Now my story...

It begins with grandparents Doug and Kathy, who contacted me and said their daughter and son-in-law, Jessica and Aaron, were coming home to visit. They asked if I would baptize their granddaughter who was born on June 6. So on July 22, 2012, we gathered at Our Redeemer Lutheran Church at Bryant, South Dakota, for the baptism of Aspen Jessica.

After the baptism, Aspen's Mom and Dad gave me an envelope. I asked if there was money in it, and if I could give their gift to ELCA World Hunger. (*Note: ELCA Good Gifts is a part of ELCA World Hunger.*) They said I could do whatever I wanted with their gift.

So that was my plan, but then the plan changed. The next weekend, July 28 and 29, I would be at Lutheran Church of Our Redeemer in Watertown, leading worship and preaching, and I would be talking to the children. I decided to share Aspen's gift with the children.

The Gospel reading was the story of the boy who shares his lunch of five loaves and two fish with Jesus. (John 6:1-14) It was the beginning of a miracle, resulting in over 5000 people being fed. I brought a bag lunch to worship, not filled with loaves and fish, but with $2 bills.

I read the story of the boy who shared his lunch and I talked about Aspen, about her baptism, and the gift from her Mom and Dad. Then, I showed her picture and opened my lunch sack filled with one hundred $2 bills.

"Is that real money?" one child asked.

I told the children about ELCA Good Gifts, how they could ask Mom and Dad to help them with the website, and how they could give a gift to help a child or family by buying a malaria net for $10, or a blanket for $10, or a duck for $20, or a pig for $30, or a goat for $50, or, my favorite, ten chicks for $10. I told them how these gifts help people in places where life is hard. Like the boy who shared his lunch, I said, you can share what you have. It may not seem like much, but it is something. Then, we said a prayer and I gave the children some of the money from Aspen. At the three services on Saturday and Sunday, I gave fifty $2 bills to twenty-four children.

I told them they could add to what Aspen gave them, so they could give a gift of a net or chicks or goat. Aspen's gift, like the boy's lunch of five loaves and two fish, could be the beginning of a miracle.

I decided at some point on Sunday to not give out the other $100 I had received from Aspen's Mom and Dad. I would send that directly to ELCA Good Gifts in honor of Aspen.

After the Saturday service at Lutheran Church of Our Redeemer, I baptized John Dean and London. The family had been in worship and heard about Aspen and her gift. After the baptism, John Dean and London's Mom and Dad gave me $50 to send to ELCA Good Gifts.

On Sunday, I baptized Alexa. After the service, Alexa's Mom and Dad gave me $20 and asked me to purchase two malaria nets in honor of their daughter. One of Alexa's grandfathers overheard our conversation, handed me $20, and told me to "make that four malaria nets." He had been in Viet Nam, and had slept under such a net almost every night.

By now, Aspen had given $100 to twenty-four children, with the hope that they would add to that and buy a Good Gift, and I still had the other $100 from Aspen, plus $50 from John Dean and London, $40 from Alexa, and $20 from Donna (this came later; read below) for a total of $210 to give to ELCA Good Gifts. The original $200 from Aspen had grown to $310.

The story continues. Following the second service that Sunday, there was a congregational meeting. Gary, who had been at the early service at the lake, came back to the church for the meeting, saw me and said, "I went home after church and bought a goat." Later I learned that Dave heard what Gary said and went home and bought an Alpaca. The next week, I visited with Phil, who has three children. He told me they were still trying to decide what they would buy. Then Donna gave my wife a $20 bill, and asked me to buy two malaria nets.

After this article appeared in our local paper, I received $20 from Aspen's grandparents and $20 from my friend, Bertha. Vivian and I decided to add $50, so $300 was sent to ELCA Good Gifts. With the $100 given to the 24 children, the original $200 had doubled to $400.

In the fall of 2012, Aspen's aunt Amy (sister to Aspen's Mom), who knew Aspen's story, went to the children at her church, American Lutheran, in De Smet, and told them about ELCA Good Gifts and a program called God's Global Barnyard. Amy began with the 5th and 6th graders. She told them how this ministry invites us to buy specific animals to give to needy families in over 60 countries to help fight poverty and hunger. Amy then went to the website and ELCA Good Gifts provided the children with barn-shaped offering boxes, which Amy said, "got the kids excited."

Then, the Church Council got involved by deciding to give half of the Advent offerings to this mission and half to the local food pantry. Amy said they also received donations from individual members of the congregation.

By Christmas, they had received $766 from the barn offering boxes, $574 from the Advent offerings, and $750 from members of the congregation.

Then, the Council designated half of the Christmas Eve offering for ELCA Good Gifts, with the other half going to the local food pantry once again. That offering for ELCA Good Gifts totaled $1,660.

By Christmas the children had raised $3,750. They used that money to purchase 4 cows, 6 sheep, 8 goats, 12 pigs, 8 ducks, and 80 chickens through ELCA Good Gifts. All those animals went to places that most of us will never see, to help families we will never meet. So it is of faith.

It is also of Jesus, who said, "for I was hungry and you gave me food..."

We ask: "Lord, when was it we saw you hungry and gave you food?"

Jesus, our king, says: "Truly, I tell you, just as you did it to one of the least of these who are members of my family, you did it to me." (Matthew 25:31-46)

What a grand privilege and joy Jesus offers us. We get to have him over for dinner just by providing a meal for someone who is hungry. It began with the Word of God, the story of Jesus and a boy who shared his lunch. But I like to think that on July 22, 2012, for me and for a few others, it all began with Aspen. Some day, I hope her Mom and Dad tell her what she started on the day she was baptized.

~

52. The Air We Breathe

I grew up in a home where we did not talk about forgiveness, or go around saying I am sorry, forgive me, or I forgive you. We were a bunch of Norwegians living together. We didn't get wordy or do a lot of hugging. But forgiveness was in the air; it was what we breathed. Our home was safe to come home to.

When I backed the car into the mailbox at the top of hill at the end of our driveway, I don't remember making a confession or either parent voicing absolution. But the car got fixed and I got to drive again, hopefully being more careful. I call that forgiveness. As a family we went to church, met Jesus, brought him home with us. We didn't talk a lot about him, but he was real.

Forgiveness is that fresh air Jesus breathes into us, in the same way God breathed into humankind the breath of life. Forgiveness is about being filled with the breath of God. Jesus says, "Receive the Holy Spirit. If you forgive the sins of any, they are forgiven them." (John 20:22-23)

So Jesus breathes forgiveness into us, and we then breathe it out into the world. The church will be that breath of fresh air in the world.

Jesus went about forgiving people, sometimes after they repented and asked to be forgiven, and sometimes without hearing any repentance at all. His forgiveness did not depend upon the actions of the receiver. Jesus knew forgiveness is necessary, so he forgave whether the other party asked for it or not.

A woman was told by her husband of twenty-three years that he loved her and was happy to be her husband, that he loved the children and wanted to continue to be their father, but that for years he had been having affairs with other women and he planned to continue doing so. He was not asking forgiveness or permission, but was just telling her. She left him. A year later she divorced him. Then she began drinking to numb the pain.

One day she decided to do two things. She quit drinking and she forgave him. He didn't ask to be forgiven, but she forgave him anyway. She said it was necessary.

Forgiveness always costs. The one who forgives pays a price, gives up something. Perhaps it is pride. The woman said it was a good thing for her. I never learned how the husband felt about it, but I would think he was surprised. It was more than he could have possibly expected.

Forgiveness is that way. It is more than we have a right to expect; therefore, the only response is thankfulness. In the case of God, praise is also appropriate.

~

53. Mowing With Our Plastic Mowers

Though indeed God is not far from each one of us. For "in him we live and move and have our being."

Acts 17:27-28

Lucas, two years old, is out mowing the yard, following behind his father with a plastic mower. Now you might think that Lucas is pretending to mow the lawn, that he is simply playing a game. But I think not. If I were to ask him what he is doing, he would most certainly answer: "I am mowing the lawn." When Dad and Lucas are done, the lawn will look quite beautiful, and Lucas will be proud of the job he has done.

We follow after Jesus with our plastic mowers. The grass gets cut. We are proud of our mowing.

54. Some Thoughts About Trust

I watched part of a movie on television and decided to purchase a DVD copy of it. The film was made in the 1940s and was not to be found at any local store or on any of the more popular Internet sites, but I finally located it on the website of a company in California. I had ordered another 'hard to find' film for my daughter from a similar website and that went well. So I placed my order, paid the bill, and waited. Ten days later I received a package with a movie inside, but not the one I had ordered.

I sent an email to the website, followed by another and yet another, but did not hear back. My assumption is I never will hear from these crooks. So I am out twenty dollars, stuck with an unwanted film and the knowledge that I was foolish. I will find it difficult to trust other unknown websites for a long time, even those that can be trusted. One has broken trust for many.

Ernest Hemingway (1899-1961) once said: "The best way to find out if you can trust somebody is to trust them." That pretty much describes me. I like to trust people and so I begin by trusting them until I find out otherwise. That has cost me. But I still want to trust every person I meet, and most of the time such trust is justified.

Frederick Buechner, in his book *Listening to Your Life*, writes about being parked by a roadside, depressed and afraid because his daughter was very ill. A car came along with a license plate that carried one word – TRUST. He asks: "What does one call a moment like that? Is it something to laugh off as a joke or coincidence, or is it a word from God?" He concludes it was a bit of both. He knows it helped.

Buechner called it an epiphany, a divine revelation from God. The owner of the car turned out to be a trust officer at a bank. He later gave the plate to Buechner, who has kept it on a bookshelf as a reminder.

A pastor was telling a group of children that God could be trusted because God is our Heavenly Father. One of the boys rebelled at the words. Later the pastor found out that the boy's father abused him, so if God is like a father, then God cannot be trusted.

We read these words in the book of Psalms: "Trust in the LORD, and do good." (Psalm 37:3) It is as if one follows the other. If I can trust, then it frees me to spend my life. I am not occupied by questions, or diverted by suspicion. I can rest back in the comfort of a safe place of trust and go out from there into the world, ready to share that trust

It is certainly more difficult to enjoy a baseball game when one spends nine innings wondering how many of the players have spent the morning shooting up rather than working out. It is certainly disheartening to hear that another person elected to high office has somehow forgotten to pay his taxes or her speeding tickets. Eventually, we quit going to baseball games and we begin to distrust all of government. Since we live in community, what each individual does affects the whole.

So, also, it is difficult for the world to look to the church for guidance and hope when it is discovered that we who are members of this body cannot be trusted.

Even though Fred Buechner was blessed by the word TRUST on the back of a passing car, we cannot expect the world to trust the church, or come to trust in God, simply by hanging the right license plates on the back of our cars.

A footnote: after I wrote these words, I contacted the Better Business Bureau in California and told them of my experience with the website selling old movies. A short time later, I received the movie I had ordered. I returned the unwanted film and enclosed a brief note that read: "Now was that so hard?"

It made me feel better.

~

55. Four Candles for Advent

<u>Candle 1: The Mary Candle</u>
Mary, who was about the age of your average high school student, was engaged – an arranged marriage – to a man named Joseph. Before the marriage, a messenger from God, an angel named Gabriel, came to Mary and told her three things:

i.   God likes you.

ii. Don't afraid.

iii. By the way, you are going to have a baby. and you are to name him Jesus.

Mary said okay, and the angel left.

When Mary was pregnant, she sang: "My whole being praises God. I am full of joy, for God has looked upon me with great favor. Me, an ordinary young girl. I am blessed and for years to come, it will be known that I am blessed. God, who is holy, has done this great thing through me. For in the name of this child, the proud and the powerful will be made low and those who are considered of no importance will be lifted up. The hungry will be fed and those who misuse their wealth will be sent to their rooms to think about what they do. But from the beginning to the end, my God always remembers mercy."

Light the first candle on the Advent wreath and remember Mary. Remember Bethlehem and Joseph, the journey, the manger, and the shepherds. Remember that God had great faith in Mary. Remember that God has great faith in you.

Candle 2: The Neighbor Candle

Jesus comes into our hearts, by faith, in the waters of Baptism, in the Bread and Wine of Holy Communion, and as we reach out to help the neighbor.

There are 300 verses in the Bible that speak of the poor and of social justice. Jesus says to us: "I was hungry and you gave me food. I was thirsty and you gave me something to drink. I was a stranger and you welcomed me. I was naked and you gave me clothing. I was sick and you took care of me. I was in prison and you visited me."

We ask: "When did we see you hungry or thirsty, when were you a stranger, and when were you poor or sick or in prison?"

Jesus answers: "As much as you did it to one of the least of these, you did it to me."

Jesus comes in the neighbor. Who is your neighbor? If someone is in need and you have the means by which to help, that someone is your neighbor.

Light the second candle on the Advent wreath and remember the neighbor.

Candle 3: The Candle of Hope

Jesus says to us: "Let not your hearts be troubled. In my Father's house there are many dwelling places. If it were not so, would I have told you that I go to prepare a place for you?"

This season of joy we call Christmas is, for many, a season of great sadness. We are reminded of those who will not be with us this Christmas.

There is still the laugher of children, the gathering with family, the surprise of an unexpected gift, the kindness of friends. But there are also tears. We miss the ones who used to share the joy of Christmas with us. The sadness is real.

Hope is also real. We hear the promise from Jesus: "I will come again and will take you unto myself, so that where I am, there you may be also." We are told of a place where every tear is wiped away and "death will be no more." Advent is about hope.

Light the third candle, the Candle of Hope, and remember the saints who no longer walk this earth with you. Say their names and give thanks to God.

Candle 4: The Jesus Candle

When you light the Mary Candle, remember the birth of Jesus.

When you light the Neighbor Candle, remember when you help the neighbor, you bump into Jesus.

When you light the Candle of Hope, remember Jesus is the one who gives us such hope.

Light the fourth candle, the Jesus Candle, and remember it's all about Jesus. From Bethlehem to Heaven, from birth to neighbor to hope, it's all about Jesus.

~

56. Another Year

Another Year is the title of a British film that came out in 2010, written and directed by Mike Leigh. It is an unusual movie because there are no car chases, no one is murdered, no mystery is solved, no aliens land on our planet in an effort to take over the world, and men aren't depicted as complete idiots.

It is a comedy and a drama, divided into four parts, with each part tied to one of the four seasons: Spring, Summer, Autumn, Winter. It is a story about a happily married couple and their family and friends. We see ordinary people over the course of one year as they go about their ordinary lives and strive to care for one another. Nothing much happens, except the birth of a child, the death and funeral of a husband's wife, the engagement of one son, the anger and estrangement of another, the efforts to help a woman who is suffering from depression, and the friendship shown to two lonely people. The viewers experience joy and insight as they listen to intelligent people having conversation.

Some will not like this movie because they will not get to watch two strangers having sex, or get to scream when very stupid young people open doors no one else in the world would open, or get to cheer on their favorite vampire. The movie does not end with a passionate embrace or a ride into the sunset. Everybody doesn't live happily ever after. It simply stops in the middle of a dinner, with the camera focused on Mary. We see the loneliness in her eyes as we hear the conversation and laughter that surround her, and wonder what will happen to her. Another year has passed; another year begins. It is called life, a grand mixture of comedy and drama.

On the CD by the Nitty Gritty Dirt Band, *Will the Circle Be Unbroken, Vol. 2*, there is a brief exchange before John Denver is to sing. He begins to strum his guitar with the band and asks, "Is this practice?" To which a band member responds, "They're all practice." So it is with life.

111

Every day is practice. We do not know perfection. We fail and we try again. Babies are born. Friends die. We go to work. We celebrate birthdays. We pray. Some days are so hard, we might wonder if it's all worth it. Other days are so full of joy, we can hardly believe how blessed we are. And all the while, through the comedy and the drama, we are held in the love of God and guided by a faith that propels us out to do good in God's world, as best we can.

Life.

What a grand gift. Another year. Another day. Another moment. Another breath.

"This is the day that the LORD has made; let us rejoice and be glad in it." (Psalm 118:24)

~

57. Sabbath

Most every Sunday morning, Stub Kaberle came to worship, found his usual pew, and almost immediately fell asleep. Stub farmed; he worked hard all week. The church was warm and comfortable and safe. Stub was there, always faithful. He gathered with family and friends in a community of faith, getting his Sabbath, resting back in the welcome comfort of Jesus.

It was just fine. I thought it high praise that in Christ's church, Stub Kaberle could sleep like a baby.

My last Sunday in that congregation, Stub sat up front, stayed awake the whole time.

That was just fine, too.

58. Parade
For princess Bernie, and her father.

A parade is coming by my house,
this blustery day in February.
I am inside,
looking out my window.
It is a short parade,
heading north.
The grand marshal is the dog,
looking quite proud.
Followed by the father,
smiling.
His right hand
attached to a wagon.
Riding in the wagon
is the princess,
all bundled,
looking about
for spectators.
I wave.
Later, but not much,
the parade is going south,
still led by the same grand marshal,
with the same father,
and the same wagon,
attached to the same right hand.
A more determined
look upon his face.
The princess
is being carried
under the father's left arm,
helpless, but secure.
Unable to wave
at this moment.

59. Unbind Him and Let Him Go

Now a certain man was ill, Lazarus of Bethany, the village of Mary and her sister Martha. (John 11:1)

He had two sisters, Martha and Mary. He lived in Bethany. He was a close friend of Jesus. His name was Lazarus.

Or his name was LeRoy or Nelda or Rick or Eileen. Each one has a story to tell. Each one leaves behind family and friends who weep.

For every picture on that obituary page in the local paper there is a Martha or a Mary, sisters or husbands or wives or parents or children or friends who mourn and question.

"Lord, if you had been here." (v. 21)

Have we not said it?

Then Martha adds, without pause or hesitation, "But even now I know that God will give you whatever you ask of him." (v. 22)

Even in the midst of death, faith comes.

Later, there will be another cave and another Mary coming in the early morning. Another stone will be rolled away and another grave will be empty. The sign of Lazarus will become something else. The sign of Lazarus will become a promise to the whole world.

"I am the resurrection and the life." Jesus says to Martha. (v. 25)

Then Jesus asks Martha: "Do you believe?"

Martha answers: "Yes, Lord, I believe." (v. 27)

When we gather for worship, we are saying: "Yes, Lord, I believe." When we place our gifts in the offering plate, we are saying: "Yes, Lord, I believe." When we bring the children to Sunday School or invite someone into our congregation, we are saying: "Yes, Lord, I believe." When we reach out to help the neighbor, we are saying: "Yes, Lord, I believe."

114

And we believe, in part, because Martha believes. It is that way. Faith comes by hearing. We believe because someone else believed and then told.

"Lazarus, come out." (v. 43)

Jesus called him by name. In Holy Baptism, your name was spoken. God remembers your name.

There will come a time when Jesus will call you by name and give the order: "Unbind her, and let her go."

~

60. The Plant

Vivian and I bought a plant. It was full and green, with a name that was long and unpronounceable. It needed water most every day, telling us this by drooping its head and losing its leaves.

The phone-call from my sister came on a Thursday. She said I needed to come home. Dad had collapsed Wednesday night and was in the hospital. We left for Washington State on Friday afternoon. At 2AM the next morning, we entered his hospital room. My sister was asleep in a chair. Dad was in bed, eyes almost closed. I greeted my sister, walked over to the bed, and touched my father's shoulder. I spoke too loudly, almost a shout in the dark quiet. He opened his eyes and saw nothing. My last conversation with him had been a phone call a week earlier. There would be no more, ever.

Dad lived one more week. He died in the night, waking us with his silence.

We had left home in a hurry, not thinking about turning off some stuff or canceling other stuff. Still, all was well when we returned. Except for the plant. Vivian took the plant to the garage. Later I went there and cut away all the brown, dry, dead parts, leaving only a little. It was enough. The plant lived. I was glad for its life.

My father did not die suddenly. His body began to shut down, part by part, each part seeming to cause death in the next part until, in the middle of the night, with a child on each side, the final breath came out of him, like a deep, deep sigh.

It is the reverse of creation, when God breathed into humankind the breath of life and created living beings. Some eighty-five years before, in a farmhouse in North Dakota, a doctor pulled my father out of his mother, slapped him on his bottom, and listened for a cry and the breath that came with it. Then, too soon, his children wait, listening for each breath, listening for the silence that will be the knowledge that the breath is gone forever.

We took his body to strangers. They did their work, so that his body looked like life. But it was only an appearance. It was not life. There was no breath. There was only silence.

In the Gospel of John, when Mary sees Jesus, whom she knows to be dead, she does not know it is Jesus. She thinks he is the gardener. In a way, she is right. God is a gardener.

~

61. A Wedding Sermon in Three Sentences

Over the years I have distilled most of my wedding sermons into three sentences. Here they are:

1. *You are blessed because you are each loved by the other.* So it might be good if every day you say a prayer of thanks to God for letting you live your life with this one person who, surprisingly enough, not only puts up with you, but also loves you. What a gift this is. How blessed you are.

2. *Loving this person you wed today is your best work.* The Bible has this four-word admonition that I believe is the foundation for your life together: "Husbands, love your wives." (Ephesians 5:25) If we do that, a host of other problems will be solved and this world will be a better place. Children will grow up safer, healthier and wiser.

3. *You are not alone.* We are gathered here in the name of God, who is Father, Son, and Holy Spirit. Our faith is that God is present. Just as Jesus came to the wedding at Cana, so he is in attendance here at your wedding. We invoke God's presence and trust God is here with you today and will be with you in your life together. But this also is true: your family and your friends are here because they care about you. Do you think these people like to go to weddings? They are here at your wedding because of their deep and abiding love for you. You are not alone. They may give you advice, whether you like it or not, and they will give you their guidance and support. Let them help you.

I usually close with the words of a gas station attendant to a couple who stopped at his business after their wedding. As they were going out the door, he said:
"Be good to each other."

62. Always

We are like the child being watched by her father as she attempts to nail a box together. With great effort and care she pounds each nail and tries to get the angles right and the sides even. When she is done, she holds the box up to her father, and he can see where she has missed and damaged the wood and where the sides are not even and how crooked it is. Then he takes the box in his big hands, holds it close to his face, looks at it all around, turns, looks down at his daughter, and says, "Perfect, just perfect."

For sure, we get it wrong.

But we are always God's children.

~

63. Sweet as Honey

He said to me, O mortal, eat what is offered to you; eat this scroll, and go, speak to the house of Israel. So I opened my mouth, and he gave me the scroll to eat. He said to me, Mortal, eat this scroll that I give you and fill your stomach with it. Then I ate it; and in my mouth it was as sweet as honey.

Ezekiel 3:1-3

Words…
   giving life
      I baptize you
      The body of Christ… The blood of Christ… for you
      Your sins are forgiven
      Jesus is risen
      The Lord bless you and keep you

   sustaining faith
      The Lord is my shepherd
      Our Father who art in heaven
      For God so loved that world
      Jesus is Lord
      Go in peace

   encouraging
      I love you
      I forgive you
      Welcome
      Well done
      Thank you
      Congratulations
      I'm sorry
      Good to see you
      Please stay
      I promise

Words… only words… but sweet as honey

64. A Tiny Christmas Poem

when next you hold a child
eyes filled with wonder like faith
tiny toes that kick for joy
remember Mary
beautiful Mary
and give thanks

65. Free as a Bird

It was early morning. I was making the school run with my two children, Christin in middle school, and Josh in grade school. We speeded to the middle school first, passing the robin on the way.

Spring had come, changed her mind, and left again, leaving some of God's creatures a bit confused. One fat robin was attempting flight after breakfast with no success.

Ice.

We passed, and tried to think of other things. After leaving Christin at her school, rather than take the usual route, Josh and I returned by way of the victim. She was still there, a wing frozen to the pavement. We passed again, considered this feathered neighbor for another block, and then made an illegal turn. We freed the robin and placed the tired and frightened creature on the floor by the car's heater.

We had an idea. Josh's teacher would know what to do. Together we entered his third grade classroom. This good teacher usually had some feathered or furry friend sharing space with the children. I left, knowing the robin was in good hands.

Josh informed me one week later that the class gathered outside in the morning sun to watch the robin fly away. Free as a bird.

A lawyer asks Jesus, "Who is my neighbor?" (Luke 10:29) In reply, Jesus tells the story of a man who is robbed and left to die by the side of the road. In turn, two people pass by, see the man, and continue on their way. A third person passes, then stops and gives aid, making sure that the wounded man's needs are met. Then Jesus asks: "Which of these three, do you think, was a neighbor to the man?" (v. 36)

Another translation (Revised Standard Version) reads: "Which of these three... proved neighbor to the man?"

One spring morning a particular robin was in need and Josh and I proved to be neighbor. It was no big deal, except to the robin.

I am sure that in this world there are many wounded robins every morning. One temptation is to consider them unimportant, another is to proclaim that if they are in trouble it is their own fault, and yet another is to become so bewildered by the number of wounded robins as to give up doing anything at all.

When God tells us to love the neighbor, God is not much interested or concerned about how we might feel about that neighbor; rather, God is telling us to do something. This love that God commands is not about a particular emotion or feeling. This love is an act of the will.

If you know of someone in need and you have the resources to help, you have something to prove to God and to yourself.

~

66. To See with New Eyes

Steven Covey, in his book *The Seven Habits of Highly Effective People* (Free Press, 2004), tells the story of being on a subway in New York on a Sunday morning. People were sitting quietly, some reading newspapers, some dozing; a peaceful, calm scene.

The subway stopped and a man and his children entered. Soon the children were yelling back and forth, throwing things, bumping into the other riders, and generally making everyone uncomfortable and angry. The father did nothing. Covey said he could not believe this man could be so insensitive as to let his children run wild.

Finally Covey told the man that the children were disturbing the other people, and asked him to please do something about it. Covey said the man seemed to be unaware of what had been going on around him. The father said he was sorry, and yes, of course he would do something. Then he explained that he and the children had just come from the hospital. His wife and the children's mother had died an hour ago.

Nothing changed in the subway, yet everything changed. Steven Covey and the other riders on that bus saw with new eyes.

A man was driving to work one morning when he had a little fender bender with another driver, a woman. They both stopped. The woman got out to survey the damage and started to cry. It was her fault, she admitted. Her car was new, two weeks old. She did not want to have to tell her husband. But things had to be done, so she went to the glove compartment to find the registration and insurance papers. As she reached in she found a paper with her husband's handwriting: "In case of an accident, remember honey, it's you I love, not the car."

This good husband wanted to make sure his wife did not get so involved in one thing that she missed out on another, so involved in a dent that she missed out on a greater truth.

She saw with different eyes and understood what was important. She knew she was loved.

Jesus' hope for the church is that we see with new eyes—to understand what is true, what has value, and what is important, to not miss out on one thing because we are so occupied with another, which is less.

I was visiting with friends who have a son who was getting married. They talked with pride about this son and his bride, about his compassion for people. He went to Tanzania some years ago and that changed him. He is the baby in the family and the rest of his siblings considered him quite spoiled, perhaps even selfish. He went to Africa for five months. He saw poverty, discrimination and hardship firsthand. His parents say he is a better person for that journey. He sees with new eyes. He sees others as Jesus sees them.

Part of worship, part of following Jesus, part of church, is to see the truth of us, to see our faults and our failings, and then to hear the news that we are loved and forgiven. Another part of worship is to sit still for a while, quit fussing about things for a few minutes, and see those who have become invisible: the poor, the powerless, the stranger, those carrying heavy burdens silently and alone. To see with Jesus' eyes is to see a world in need of attention, in need of care.

A part of worship is to see that we, who are so blessed, have responsibilities. I am guessing that you and I have been blessed by God more than we ever dreamed possible. Jesus is trying to get our attention; he is trying to get us to see with new eyes, his eyes—to see the person who feels she has become invisible, to finally see her. And then to have the courage to ask, "Can I help you?"

It is as simple and as hard as that.

~

67. A Song for Three Advents

Twice born from the earth:
cave and grave,
darkness and light,
cry and shout,
blindness and sight.

Water on lace,
crumbs on wood,
smell of joy and wine,
planting trees and words,
adding one to ninety and nine.

Faith discarded,
hope tossed aside,
useless candles, obsolete,
love perfected,
image clear, complete.

68. Worship

I am in worship on a Sunday morning. The boy in the pew ahead is showing his mother that his tooth is about to come out. The young couple, just to the right of them, lean into each other, enjoying their nearness, while a gentleman to the left is barely keeping his eyes open. And what about me? Well, I am looking about, thinking I might write this down. We are God's children, gathered and undisciplined, easily distracted, but safe for this hour in a place we call a sanctuary.

69. What If We Talked with Adults

What if we talked with adults
in the same way we talk to children?
What if we said, my how big you have gotten!
Or, on your birthday, how old will you be then?

When we talk with adults,
we ask, where do you work? Do you like your new car?
What if we asked, what makes you sad?
Or looked them in the eye and said, how beautiful you are.

When we talk with adults,
we talk about what shows on the outside.
Children, still new, still learning to pretend,
are not so concerned about their pride or your pride.

Children ask the honest questions,
speak what is on their minds,
don't really know how to cover up,
hide the truth, shut the blinds.

Jesus desires we come like children,
not meaning we cast away the years,
dispense with wisdom that comes from living.
Rather, we tell the truth, speak even of our fears.

So be the child! Cry when you are hurting.
Tell another you may have lost your way,
that you are not so sure about yourself;
could use some help to get through the day.

70. Pine Box

He told his four children
to put him in a pine box.
When he was young,
he dreamed of buying a Cadillac,
but he always drove a Chevy.
When he was old and done,
a pine box was good enough.
As was the Chevy.

71. Life in Slow Motion

1956.
High school gym class.
I reached up to
the top shelf of my locker
to find something else.
I had forgotten
they were there.
So I watched, helpless,
as they fell to the cement floor.
Like in a movie, in slow motion.
We were not wealthy.
But the glasses were necessary.
The teacher said so.
They meant the giving up
of something else.
I still remember
the falling glasses.
It was my fault.
Yet I had no doubt,
I would be forgiven.
In that way,
we were wealthy.

72. Taking a Chance

The story is found in Luke's gospel, chapter 5.
Jesus is teaching near the Lake of Gennesaret. The people begin to crowd into him. It is getting difficult to concentrate, so he glances around and sees two boats, with the owners nearby cleaning their nets. Jesus gets into one of the boats, which happens to belong to Simon.

Simon jumps in, wondering what is going on, until Jesus asks him to row out into the water a bit.

Then Jesus sits down in the boat and continues to teach. When he is finished, Jesus says to Simon, "Let's go out into the deeper water and see if we can catch some fish." Simon responds politely: "You need to know up front that we have been fishing all night and nothing."

Simon is saying: I am a fisherman, and this is what I do. I know what I am doing. I have been out here all night fishing and I have nothing to show for it. Now you tell me to go out and try again. I am tired, I am empty-handed, and I don't think this will work.

Still Simon says, "Yet if you say so, I will let down the nets." (Luke 5:5)

Well, they give it one more try and they catch so many fish the nets start to tear. Simon calls out to his fishing friends to get in the other boat and give them a hand. Before they are done, both boats are filled with fish and riding low in the water.

The story is about not giving up, about trying one more time. It's about risk, about taking a chance.
It's about faith. In God. In yourself.

Be still. Listen. Jesus is speaking. *Let's go into the deeper water and see...*

129

73. Normal is Just a Setting on a Washing Machine

Only about ten percent of the world's population is left-handed, yet of the seven U.S. presidents since 1974, five are left-handed. Those five are: Gerald Ford (38), Ronald Reagan (40), George H. W. Bush (41), William Jefferson Clinton (42), and Barack Obama (44). The two right-handed gentlemen are Jimmy Carter (39) and George W. Bush (43).

Some other left-handed people you may have heard about: Babe Ruth, Bill Gates, Jimi Hendrix, Neil Armstrong, Leonardo da Vinci, Albert Einstein and Paul McCartney.

It is thought, though not proven, that left-handed people have a bit higher IQ and are more likely to excel in sports. Yet, as recently as the 1940s and '50s there have been teachers who forced left-handed students to write with their right hands by tying their left hands behind their backs. Some students were paddled on their left hand in order to convert them. To write with the left hand was considered unnatural. The left-handed person was thought to be abnormal.

When I began my studies at seminary, our national church did not allow women to be pastors. There are passages in the Bible that are pretty clear about women keeping silent in the church. But a few women joined our seminary classes anyway. At that time they were doing something women were not supposed to do, something abnormal. Later we, the church, changed our mind, in part because of those first few brave women who felt called by God. How blessed we are now to have many good pastors serving the church of Jesus Christ, who just happen to be women.

Philip Yancey, in his book *Soul Survivor*, writes of growing up in Georgia in the 1960s, and of a pastor who "preached blatant racism from the pulpit. Dark races are cursed by God, he said, citing an obscure passage in Genesis. They function well as servants... but never as leaders." (Waterbrook Press, 2003)

In other words: "They are less, they are abnormal."

There are children in our families, in our communities, in our churches who are made to feel they are less because they are homosexual. They are considered, by some, to be abnormal. Archbishop emertius Desmond Tutu of South Africa, in a sermon preached in Southwark Cathedral in London in 2004, said, "… black people were being blamed and made to suffer for something we could do nothing about—our very skins. It is the same with sexual orientation. It is a given."

The movie Temple Grandin (2010) tells the story of a woman who is autistic, who did not learn to talk until she was four years old, who was teased in school for her 'strange' behavior, and who went on to graduate from college, and to earn a Masters and a Ph.D. She has written three books and now teaches at a university. She is a celebrity, but growing up she was considered abnormal. In the film, she says her Mom and her teachers along the way "knew I was different but not less." She also says: "I know there are a lot of things I can't understand, but I still want my life to have meaning."

I have three sisters, so there are four siblings. We are very different from one another, yet none of us is less. We are family. God created us an infinite variety.

So what's normal?

Well, normal is just a setting on a washing machine.

~

74. A Shrub

The kingdom of heaven is like a mustard seed that someone took and sowed in his field; it is the smallest of all the seeds, but when it has grown it is the greatest of shrubs and becomes a tree, so that the birds of the air come and make their nests in its branches.

Matthew 12:31-32

Mustard flower, image courtesy of Leo Michels

The mustard seed never becomes a tree like an oak, maple or cedar. It grows to be eight to ten feet tall, but it is still a shrub. It will always be a shrub.

But a shrub can be home and shelter for every kind of bird.

The shrub may not tower, may not be of such great beauty, may not look strong and majestic.

But it does welcome. Every kind of bird.

So this is my prayer: May the Church of Jesus Christ be a shrub. May every congregation be a shrub.

~

75. A Child's Surprise at Christmas

I have been blessed with many Christmas gifts over the years, but the one that created the dearest memory was the gift I received when I was child.

We opened our gifts on Christmas Eve, only after supper was eaten, dishes washed, the family settled before the tree. The opening of gifts was done with ritual and in good order. But that year I could not wait for the supper and the dishes; I could not even wait for the day. It was the day before Christmas Eve and I could wait no longer.

I had asked for only one thing that year, a cap gun with belt and holster. It was necessary, for I did not simply listen to their exploits on the radio and see them ride at the picture show; I *was* Roy Rogers and the Lone Ranger and Straight Arrow. I needed that gun.

The package was there, under the tree. I knew it was the package I needed to open. I was without shame in my begging on the day before Christmas Eve. I promised I would only open one gift. I promised I would not ask for anything else. I promised to be quiet throughout supper and dishes, and I would not complain about the slowness of adults when time really counted for something.

Please, just this one package. In my heart, I knew I could be armed before nightfall. With a sigh and a smile, Mom gave permission, but reminded me of my promise. Only one. I went directly to the wrapped package that held the gift of my dreams and slowly opened it.

"Sorry," said the big bold letters on the box. It was a game called Sorry™. The irony of that title was lost on me at the time, but in later years I have come to find it appropriate. "Sorry," said the gift.

I was fooled. My mother did not laugh or lecture. She did make some comment about judging a book by its cover, whatever that meant, and she did remind me of my promise.

We are fooled often by appearances, and I suppose there is a lesson here. But I'd rather tell you of a surprise, for it is surprise that makes the memory still sweet after all the years. You see, on Christmas Eve that year, there was another package and inside was a white jeweled belt with holster and in the holster a white handled six-shooter.

To be sure, we are surprised by the choices we make, the words we speak too quickly, and the deeds we do too selfishly. But Christmas is not about those surprises, nor about a god who is making a list and checking it twice to find out who is naughty and who is nice. Rather Christmas is the surprise that God comes, born of woman, a baby to be held. God so comes to live in this world, to know us and to have compassion for us. Such is the kindness of God, and we are surprised by it over and over again.

~

76. The Light is Better

A man is seen late at night, walking in slow circles below a streetlight, looking down. Another gentleman comes by and asks if he needs help. The first man answers that he is looking for his billfold. The second man asks: "Did you lose it close to this lamp post?"

"No, I lost my billfold over there." He points down the block into the darkness.

"Then why are you looking over here?"

"Well," says the first man, "the light is better over here."

I am angry at a friend, but I do not wish to hurt his feelings, so I say nothing. Then one day I say something to my wife in a joking way, but it is also a criticism and there is anger under the humor. The moment I say the words I know I wanted to say those words to the friend, but it is easier to say them to my wife. The light is better.

We do this. We yell at our children when we want to yell at our boss. We take it out on a co-worker when we are having trouble at home. We express frustration with a friend when we are really frustrated with ourselves.

Because the light is better…

It is easier.

But the truth is never found.

~

77. One Day when Making Lefse with my Wife

The pain began in my left arm, a slight ache, nothing sharp or unbearable, but it continued. We drove to the emergency room. Within a few hours, my good doctor said he did not believe I was having a heart attack, but something was very wrong. He sent me to a heart doctor, who said a virus had decided to take up residence in that part of my body.

I spent ten days in the hospital. It was 1995.

I had met Arve twenty years before, when we served churches a few miles apart in southeast South Dakota. Arve came to see me in the hospital. There is little I remember about his visit, but as he was leaving, he came to the side of my bed, leaned down, and gently kissed me on the forehead.

I remember the kiss not as offensive or something to laugh about, but as a sacred moment. It was indeed a holy kiss. No words were spoken and no explanation was necessary. Arve was a messenger, an angel sent to deliver God's kiss. I still lay sick and would remain so for some time, but I was not forgotten by friends or by God.

A sign had been given to me.

I have never heard a booming voice from heaven or had a vision in the night, but I have, as you have, received small signs. In the midst of the troubles and the chaos, there appears sheer goodness, unexpected, even tiny, delivered by another human being, another broken sinner. Like the hand of a newborn child: small, helpless, and perfect. You are able to smile again and hope again; you want to believe and do believe that God is good and knows you need a kiss.

~

78. He Asks Not
(For Jim Boline, pastor and friend)

He asks not for our success,
nor our power.
He looks not for great achievements,
nor victory.
He seeks not our fine ideas,
nor our wisdom.
He bids us follow him,
and then turns–face set–and goes to Jerusalem.

79. I Wish for You Laughter

If I am not allowed to laugh in heaven, I don't want to go there.

Martin Luther

When Vivian and I first moved to Watertown, we purchased a house that faced the street with a garage that faced the alley. When coming home, I would make a right turn into the alley and then almost immediately make a left turn into the driveway and the garage. Leaving, I would back out of the garage and at the end of the short driveway, make a turn into the alley and then enter the street. To drive fast was to cross the alley and plow into the neighbor's house.

In short, there was no space in which to gain speed. In turn, this meant that I would spend a good portion of the winter stuck in our driveway, either coming or going. But even with that knowledge born of several winters, each new snow would bring with it the conviction that this time I can make it, this time it will be different. It is a deficiency in thinking that most men seem to carry and pass on to their sons.

It was a Sunday morning. Snow had fallen most of the night. I knew I could make it this time. I got about twenty feet. It was just far enough to be parked in the alley, so I needed to get the car back into the garage. Vivian heard me shoveling and came out to help. The early morning silence was broken by the sounds of shovels meeting snow, a few grunts and some soft muttering. We got the car into the garage.

Vivian looked at the clear sky, the sun beginning to shine, and the amount of snow that needed to be shoveled, and said, "You know, it's not too bad out here. There's no wind. It's going to be a clear, sunny day. I think you could walk."

Now you know that walking with snow is different from walking without snow. Without snow, a person can walk the way God intended people to walk. With snow, all the rules change.

138

If the snow is deep, and this was deep, there is a very definite kind of lifting of the leg and putting it down again. This is not fast walking. If there is a vehicle track, and there was, you can decide to put one foot in the track and leave the other out, so half your body is moving quickly and the other half is trying to catch up. The third option is to put both feet in the track and pretend you are a tightrope walker.

I tried all of the above methods for a block or two, and then it came to me like an epiphany. The one who had announced: "It's not so bad out here," was not here. She was back in bed, cozy warm. The one who said: "I think you can walk," was nowhere to be seen, much less walking.

I discovered that day that one can walk faster when angry.

In the book of Genesis, there is a beautiful story of Abraham and Sarah. They are both old, well past the time of bearing and raising children. God promises they will have a son. Sarah laughs at the idea. God keeps the promise. Mom and Dad name their son Isaac, which in Hebrew means "laughter." When they hold "Laughter" in their arms, they know the goodness of God.

Theologian Karl Barth (1886-1968) said, "Laughter is the closest thing to the grace of God."

My wish for you, dear reader, is laughter.

Every day.

~

80. The Light in Howard's Eyes

We were coming home on the bus, as we did every afternoon, from the high school in town to our homes in the country. The trips to and from school provided ample opportunity for telling stories, teasing the girls, laughing at stupid jokes, and getting into fights.

Howard was my best friend then. He lived close by and we spent a lot of time together, doing nothing of great importance but having a great time. We never fought, except for this one terrible day.

Try as I may, I cannot remember what it was all about. It never came to blows. It was just a lot of yelling and shaking of fists. Not so much at first, because we were still on the bus and the driver could get real mean, but then we got off the bus. I got off first. Howard got off right behind me. The stop was between our homes, so he had to go right and I always headed left.

I hit the ground, mad and afraid, turned left and kept moving. I wanted this to be done, now. But he didn't turn right. He followed behind me, words flying, and the bus driver was already too far away to hear or care anymore.

It was then that I turned. I remember that turn. I remember the dust from the bus on the gravel. I remember the smell of the air, because air always smelled better when I was a kid. I remember the afternoon sun hitting my eyes when I turned and spoke words so as to hurt, even destroy my friend.

My words stopped his mouth and took the light out of his eyes. Whenever we played, told each other jokes, or teased the girls, there was always this kind of light in Howard's eyes.

He was always smiling. It made me happy to be with him. He made me smile. He gave me courage. He was my friend, and I was stronger, braver, and even smarter when I was with him.

But now I was scared and I was mad, so I opened my mouth and told him I hated him. I told him he would never be my friend anymore.

It was one thing to disagree, even argue, even yell, but this was something else. I changed things forever.

There was no forgiveness to tell you about now. There was no happy ending. There was no resurrection.

Only this one Good Friday…

So you say, no big deal, just two kids having a schoolyard fight. But what came out of my mouth, out of my heart and soul, had power. I used that power to hurt, to destroy, even to kill.

I know, because I saw the light go out Howard's eyes.

~

81. One Mother
For Koyla Kruse

She has three boys. When she was pregnant for the fourth time, she found herself praying, please God, not another boy. She was immediately sorry to have prayed such a prayer, but it was, in that moment, the truth of her. She was tired.

Her fourth child is a girl, living under the protection of the three brothers and bringing some calm to the storm.

She tells the story of discovering that one of her sons had done something he was not supposed to do. She took hold of his arm, pulled him to her with the intention of having a conversation, mostly one-sided. He must have thought that something more than talk was going to take place, because as she was pulling him toward her, he pleaded: "Spanking don't show grace. Spanking don't show grace."

She said it was hard to reprimand this child of hers who has such a good understanding of Christian theology.

~

82. Good Friday

Jesus once said to a man: "Son, your sins are forgiven."
"Blasphemy," they said. "Why does this fellow speak in this
way? Who can forgive sins but God alone? Are you then the Son
of God?"
"You say that I am," he said.

He spoke of a kingdom unlike any other kingdom, where
children are welcome and the language of forgiveness is spoken
everyday. He had conversation with women as if they were as
important as men, and he sat at table with people usually not
invited to dinner. And, to the ears of some, he spoke blasphemy.
His fate was sealed.

When he was about the age of 33, he set his face toward
Jerusalem. He did not go there determined to die, but he knew
the truth of it, the possibility, perhaps even the certainty of his
dying. Those who landed on Omaha Beach in 1944, and those
who marched from Selma to Montgomery in 1965, and Martin
Luther King when he went to Memphis in 1968 – they all knew
they might be killed. So Jesus knew. He remembered the stories
of the prophets put to death in Jerusalem, because they spoke
against oppression and injustice. He was one of them. So he
went to Jerusalem.

There is something about us that does not like the
unconditional love of God when it is directed at those we deem
unworthy, a love that welcomes the Prodigal home, goes out
looking for one lost sheep, or prays for one's enemies.

So, we will do away with such love. We will nail him to a
cross and be done with him.

But even there, on that cross, he will not be done with us.
For his words embrace us, teach us, fill us with sadness, and yet
with great hope.

So he prays for us: "Father, forgive them." So he promises
us: "You will be with me." So he cares for us: "Woman, here is
your son." So he questions, as we question: "My God, why?"

143

So he hungers and thirsts as we hunger and thirst: "I am thirsty." So he finishes his work for us: "It is finished." And finally, he trusts in God, as he would will us to trust in God: "Into your hands."

And then he breathed his last, as we will...

~

83. Betty

Betty was dying. For many years she was reminded on a regular basis that she had cancer. She would defeat it in one part of her body and then this enemy would attack another part. She met each assault with determination, with faith and hope. She won battles so often I began to think she would defeat this enemy altogether.

But then the cancer came with a vengeance. Always before, she returned home from her hospital stay and went about life. This time she went to her son's house. Hospice was called. She spent her days on the living room couch. She still talked about winning, but the fight looked to be out of her.

I went to her, bringing small talk, simple prayers, and the sacrament of Holy Communion. She was always thankful and I always left feeling helpless.

Then the phone call came from her family.

"Please come."

I went. Betty was in the bedroom. She was so weak she had not spoken to her family since morning. I told her who I was and asked if she wanted to receive the Lord's Supper. With great effort, she said: "Yes, please."

I spoke to her the words of Jesus.

"This is my body, given for you, Betty. This is my blood, shed for you." I brought the bread and the wine to her lips, like a parent feeding a child, and she took the thin wafer and the tiny sip of wine into her mouth. Then Betty turned to lay her head on the pillow, let out a breath, and died.

Her son said she was determined to live until I came. I think she lived to taste once more the food of God, and I happened to be her waiter.

The film *The Green Mile* is about guards at a state prison, and the men they execute. The cement path to the electric chair is called the green mile. At the end of the film, the narrator, one of the guards, reminds us that we all have a green mile to walk.

145

Each of the three men executed in the story is allowed a final meal, a last supper of their choosing.

The Lord's Supper is a meal for dying people, a meal for all of us. It was the meal Betty desired before she left this world.

It is meager fare, a thin tasteless wafer and a small swallow of wine, but God knows that we who are flesh and bone need nourishment. Sometimes we need something other than words. I have known some who could no longer hear the gospel, but could still taste the goodness of God in Holy Communion, the Supper of our Lord.

This meal kept them, until they could believe again.

~

84. When I Came Into This World

when i came into this world
i awakened in a crowded room
a noisy room
full of relatives
two parents
two sets of grandparents
aunts
uncles
cousins
i was constantly bumping into family
hearing about family
visiting family
but even before i took my first steps
two grandparents left
i was too young to notice
for 35 years the room was full
then my mom left
i did not think it possible
then her parents
the aunts
the uncles
my father
it is something i will not
grow accustomed to
this leaving the room
this disappearing
this going away
forever and forever
the room is not crowded now
never will be again
i am not liking the quiet

85. Ruth Ann, I'm Doing the Best I Can

Frank is gone now, left this world in 2006, and I still miss him. He and Ruth Ann became our good friends when we lived in Vermillion, South Dakota, from 1980 to 1994. The memory I share with these words is from a time the four of us—me, Vivian, Frank, Ruth Ann—were together in Sioux Falls for a church meeting.

It was a Friday in June, late evening. The business for the day had ended. We decided to go out for some ice cream at one of the Dairy Queens. For reasons now forgotten, Vivian rode with Frank and Ruth Ann, and I drove our car. Somehow, now also forgotten, I got in the middle of the Friday night "cruising the loop" traffic, and it took some time to get to our destination. I got separated from Frank's car, but we eventually met at the Dairy Queen, enjoyed the ice cream and conversation, and went our separate ways.

On the way back to our hotel, Vivian told me that they too had wandered aimlessly, like the people of Israel trying to find the promised land, through a maze of neon-lighted automobiles, sounding horns, and teenagers giving every evidence of not being bored.

She went on to say that during their search for the elusive Dairy Queen, Ruth Ann, as any good spouse is born to do, began to give Frank detailed instructions on how to turn at the right time, stop here, go slower now, faster now, and you missed the last street. I tend to believe this need to give one's soul mate these kinds of instructions while sharing an automobile is in the genes. One is born with it; it cannot be helped. This compulsion is like the need to walk and talk. It does not happen right away, but it will come.

Finally, Frank, who is a good and patient man and loves his wife dearly, said in a rather tired and perhaps excited voice:

"Ruth Ann, I'm doing the best I can."

148

Vivian and I cherish the friendship of these two lovely people. We also cherish the gift they gave us years ago one June evening in Sioux Falls, while wandering in the wilderness. Every once in awhile, when Vivian is helping me, guiding, instructing, reminding, I will turn to her and say, in a voice both tired and excited:

"Ruth Ann, I'm doing the best I can."

Now, through me, this can be Frank and Ruth Ann's gift to you. Whenever your good spouse, or your kind and gentle boss, or a helpful co-worker, or a protecting parent, or an even more protecting child, or your 'smarter than you' friend, or your anxious pastor or priest, or the ever remarkable member of your congregation who understands that everything would work much better if you will do it this way, and do it now…

Whenever you have a desire and/or need to respond to any of these helpful people, simply say:

"Ruth Ann, I'm doing the best I can."

Ruth Ann will be pleased.

~

86. The Request

By chance we met on the street.
I asked how he was doing.
She wanted me to slow down, he said.
She wanted me to sit with her, talk with her,
be with her.
I didn't have time.
I had too much to do, he said.
Now I sit.
Alone, he said.

~

87. Blessing

I went to visit her, this once intelligent, wise, kind, and beautiful woman. Now her speech was babble, her eyes filled with confusion and fear. I did not know what to do or say, so I stood, like a fool, and simply looked at her. Then I did the only thing I knew to do. I blessed her. I placed my hand upon her head and spoke the old, old words of blessing. "The Lord bless you and keep you. The Lord make his face to shine upon you and be gracious to you. The Lord look upon with favor and give you peace. In the name of the Father and of the Son and of the Holy Spirit." And so I marked the cross upon her forehead. Her eyes softened, became less fearful, and in a strong, clear, calm voice, she said, "Amen."

88. Washing Feet

Then Jesus poured water into a basin and began to wash the disciples' feet and to wipe them with the towel that was tied around him.

John 13:5

It was a task
done by the servant
in this desert place.
But on this night,
it is the teacher
who wraps a towel
around his waist,
takes a basin of water,
kneels on the floor,
going from disciple to disciple,
a smile on his face,
full of love for these men,
full of joy for what he
is doing for them.
Cleansing them.
Loving them.
Near to each one.

Kasturba washes Ghandi's feet.

89. Greatest in the Kingdom

Jesus was asked: "Who is the greatest in the kingdom of heaven?" In answer to his own question, he beckons a child and says: "Truly I tell you, unless you change and become like children, you will never enter the kingdom of heaven. Whoever becomes humble like this child is the greatest in the kingdom of heaven." (Matthew 18:1, 3-4)

We tell people to grow up. Jesus tells us to become children again.

In church, when adults enter, we give them a bulletin with announcements and an 'order' of worship. When children come in, we give them a bag filled with paper, crayons, and toys. The adults hear a sermon. The children are told stories.

Adults say it is better to give than to receive, but children have a different opinion. Adults protest: "Oh, you shouldn't have." The child asks: "Do you have anything else for me?"

Adults may be able to explain the concept of grace, but have trouble living it. Children get grace. They may not be able to explain it, but they bask in it.

Adults say "You have to believe," as if it were possible to manufacture faith. Adults make faith into a work, something to accomplish. Children enjoy believing, are naturals at it. They love to believe. Children have no trouble in believing in that which they cannot see.

I recently watched a beautiful two-year-old girl as she came running across the floor of the gathering area in our church. She had a big smile on her face and her eyes were bright with joy. She ran and ran, almost unable to contain her happiness. I turned to see where she was going, and there waiting for her was her grandfather. She almost leaped into his arms. Such was the love between these two.

The child is saying, this is my grandpa and he loves me. Be the child. Let God love you.

90. Belonging

Jesus answered, "I have told you, and you do not believe.
The works that I do in my Father's name testify to me; but you
do not believe, because you do not belong to my sheep. "

John 10:25-26

We are used to hearing, even saying: "If you will believe as we believe, then you can belong with us; you can be a part of us, be a part of our community."

In other words, believing comes first. Believe and then you can belong.

Which also means that if you do not believe, you cannot belong.

Jesus seems to be saying something else. Tag along with me, and let's see what happens. Be a part of my community. Maybe faith will come.

In other words, belonging comes first. Belonging may lead to believing.

It works for children...

91. Note of Thanks

This is a note to say thanks
to the lovely young lady
on the bike trail,
who brought unexpected joy
to our evening walk.
As you rode by, you greeted us:
"Good morning!"
I then checked my watch
to confirm what I knew,
that it was 8:59
in the evening.
I quickly attempted
to correct you:
"Good morning?"
Just as quickly, you responded:
"No. Good afternoon."
Too soon you reached
only shouting distance,
so I yelled, with a smile:
"It is nearly 9 o'clock in the evening."
It was than we heard you giggle.
This is to thank you for that giggle,
as you continued your ride
into our memories.

92. Evidence of God

But Thomas (who was called the Twin), one of the twelve, was not with them when Jesus came. So the other disciples told him, "We have seen the Lord." But he said to them, "Unless I see the mark of the nails in his hands, and put my finger in the mark of the nails and my hand in his side, I will not believe."
John 20:24-25

My grandfather was fifty miles from Mount St. Helens when it erupted in 1980. He said it was the most beautiful thing he had ever seen. Some will say: "When I look up at the stars, see the wonder of those lights in the night sky, I am even more convinced there is a God." Some will say: "When I climb to the top of a mountain, see the grandeur of creation, my faith is restored." Some will say: "When I saw my baby born, when I held her in my arms and counted each of her fingers and toes, I knew that God must be real."

Thomas says "I must see the wounds."
This is my God:
at times angry,
at times hungry,
at times praying,
at times wondering,
at times doubting,
at times thirsty.

This is my God:
telling stories,
blessing children,
eating with friends,
weeping,
bleeding,
dying,
rising.

I must see the wounds.

155

93. Questions for God and Noah

God, what did you see in Noah,
to call him righteous,
blameless?
Was there not found one other
such as he?
Obedient builder,
zoo keeper,
caring for his family?
One?
You could only find one?
And Noah, how could you
stand on that boat
and watch your neighbors
drown?

94. The Gift of Faith

In his book *Soul Survivor* (Waterbrook Press, 2003), Philip Yancey tells a story that took place in the early 1960s, in those first days of school integration in the South.

It is the story of a six-year-old girl named Ruby Bridges, the first black child to attend the Franz School in New Orleans. Each day she would walk into school, escorted by federal marshals, through a mob of white people screaming obscenities, yelling threats, and waving their fists at her.

Ruby Bridges at 6 years old.

Dr. Robert Coles, a psychiatrist and pediatrician, got to know Ruby, became her friend, and asked her how she could do it. She told him that she prayed. She prayed for herself so she would be strong and unafraid, and she prayed for her enemies, that God would forgive them.

"Jesus prayed that on the cross," she said. "Forgive them, because they do not know what they are doing."

So she prayed that prayer for those who met her with anger and hatred.

What faith can do is make a six-year-old child brave beyond her years, brave beyond our imagination. Ruby said she prayed for her enemies because that is what Jesus did. Six-year-old Ruby Bridges faced a world as broken and angry as one cannot imagine, by trusting in Jesus.

With faith, she prayed and she walked.

Faith is not our gift to God. Faith is God's gift to us. Be glad for it.

95. In Remembrance

The Lord Jesus on the night when he was betrayed took a loaf of bread, and when he had given thanks, he broke it and said, "This is my body that is for you. Do this in remembrance of me." In the same way he took the cup also, after supper, saying, "This cup is the new covenant in my blood. Do this, as often as you drink it, in remembrance of me."

1 Corinthians 11:23-25

It was the corner drug store in Rugby, North Dakota. I was 10 years old. My Mom was 31. Just inside the door was the comic book rack and straight ahead was the soda fountain. We would walk past the shelves filled with bottles of medicine, beauty aids, bandages and toothpaste, back to three booths planted against the wall. It was cool back there in the summertime and still, like some sacred place. It was a place of soft voices and polite conversation. Two glasses of water would be placed before us. My Mom would order. There was no need to ask me. She knew. A chocolate malt for me and a dish of ice cream for her. I would smile. The malt would come in a tall sweating silver container, and there was a shorter glass set down beside it, filled to the brim. We would talk, my Mom and me, the malt between us. When I drink a chocolate malt today, the memory comes back. It is more than the memory of ice cream and chocolate and malt; it is the memory of my mother. I can almost see her again across the table, hear her gentle voice, see her smile, and I remember once again her love for me.

It was an ordinary time, yet one which has taken on a significance that raises all the props and scenery of that long-ago time to a higher place. They are holy–that time and that place–not because they are in and of themselves holy, but because of what happened, because of the peace and quiet joy, and the kindness of those moments.

96. September Comes

A sweet child is coming.
She runs and puts a hug around my legs,
leans her upper body back
to show off her new earrings,
smiling up at me,
while her sister and the babysitter wait patiently.
After telling me about her trip to the mall,
she lets go of my legs, walking backwards to
get in as much talk as possible.
She waves, then turns and falls in with her sister.
I watch as she skips into the sun,
then become afraid.
I think of her summer ending,
going off to places where new
words are heard from
the mouths of God's children,
and the comfort of a mother's lap must wait
until the yellow bus brings her home.
Will she soon hide inside,
like my friend from long ago,
who with sad eyes, said,
When people tell you, you are an Indian, in such a way
to make you feel ashamed of who you are, worthless,
a lie told over and again so that finally it becomes the
only truth that matters.
So said my friend, looking down.
A sweet man.

97. The Widow's Might

Jesus sat down opposite the treasury, and watched the crowd putting money into the treasury. Many rich people put in large sums. And a poor widow came, and put in two copper coins, which are worth a penny. Then he called his disciples to him, and said to them, "Truly, I tell you, this poor widow has put in more than all those who are contributing to the treasury. For all of them have contributed out of their abundance; but she out of her poverty has put in everything she had, all she had to live on."

Mark 12:41-44

In the Greek language, the word widow means "empty." The woman is empty and yet she gives.

When someone would ask for help with a drinking problem, I would call another alcoholic, someone who belonged to AA, who was no longer drinking, but understood what it means to be empty.

When someone lost a spouse, I would find another who had lost a spouse, who understood what it is to be empty, and invite him or her to help.

The widow puts in two small copper coins, which are worth a penny. It is not enough to make a real difference in her life. It may meet her needs for a day, but not enough for tomorrow and not enough to change her status, to make her independent. Even if she kept the two copper coins, she would still be poor.

But those two coins give her, for this one day, some pride, and some evidence that she, too, has something to offer. So see her, not hanging back in the shadows, ashamed, but walking up to the offering box with dignity and with thankfulness to God that her gift is honored.

We make people feel guilty for being poor. I heard someone say that poor does not mean dirty or stupid or mean. But we sometimes make the poor feel they are not really a part of us.

Their place is to be helped, not to be the helper. This widow crossed over a line, went from being helped to being a helper. There is a joy in that.

Jesus does not stop the woman from putting in all that she has. Rather he points her out and praises her.

What does faith look like? Faith looks like a poor widow, a person who is considered empty, walking up to the offering box, putting in all she has, holding her head high.

~

98. Shame

I was asked by a family, through the local funeral home, to conduct the funeral service for a man who did not belong to our congregation. Could the family use our building and would I lead the service? The man was Native American, as were most of the family and friends who attended the service.

After the journey to the cemetery, we returned to the church for a meal. As we entered the fellowship hall, a young Indian man began questioning me, asking me who I thought I was, conducting this funeral. He was angry with me and I didn't understand why. He didn't know me. I began to realize that he was angry because I was a white man. His grandmother finally came to my rescue.

Shame on him.

A short time later, I attended a recital of classical music. During the intermission, I stepped outside. When I came back, the music had started once again, so I waited outside the recital hall until the piece was completed. Standing near me, just outside the door, was a young woman, listening with full attention to the music on the other side of the door. She was a Native American woman. I watched her and came to the realization that she understood and appreciated this music much more than I ever could. But in that same moment I realized something else. I realized I was surprised by that truth.

Shame on me.

~

99. The Christmas Letter

Vivian and I received another Christmas card on January 7. What a joy! This annual exchange of news and pictures is one of the gifts of the Christmas season, giving evidence that people can still write in full sentences. We get to hear about a baby born, a trip taken, a new place reached in the journey called life. But, best of all, the cards and letters remind us that we are remembered and loved.

There are more photos on our refrigerator this year than ever before of sleeping or confused newborn babies, old classmates surrounded by grandchildren, families at the beach or sitting at a picnic bench, weddings, family reunions, and graduations.

I share with you one Christmas letter we received this year:

To My Christian Friends—my sisters and brothers in humanity,

The day of the Holy Birth of Christ is approaching. It is truly a day of celebration for all those who believe in His message—Christians, Muslims, and many other religions. His birth heralded an era of understanding, tolerance, love, and forgiveness. Understanding achieves tolerance, tolerance breeds love, and love leads to forgiveness.

May the teaching of Jesus Christ be incarnated in our present life so that understanding, tolerance, love, and forgiveness prevail in our treatment of our fellow human beings to eradicate wars, destruction, poverty, and above all, greed. Greed is the cause of all man-made disasters on our cherished Earth.

Let us pray together and hope for the best in this Holy Season.

My family and I wish you and all your loved ones A VERY MERRY CHRISTMAS AND A HAPPY NEW YEAR. May all your dreams and hopes be fulfilled.

God bless you all.

163

The letter is from Adnan, who is married to Faye, who is a child of South Dakota, daughter to Howard and Nelda Thompson. They live on the small island nation of Bahrain, connected by a 16-mile causeway to Saudi Arabia. Adnan is Palestinian and a Muslim, a follower of Islam. I know very little about Islam or what it means to be a Muslim. But I am learning.

I am learning that Islam teaches there is one God, the same God I believe in, the God of Abraham and Moses and Jesus. Since God is one and cannot be divided, there is no Trinity. I am learning that Islam teaches that Jesus is a great prophet of God, as great as Muhammad, but Jesus is not God's Son, was not crucified, and did not die, but he ascended into heaven.

I am learning that Muslims focus on daily worship, ethics, and action. I recently read a quote from the prophet Muhammad: "If you see an evil, correct it with your hands. If you cannot, then with your tongue, and if you cannot do even that, then with your heart."

I am learning that Muslims are to "devote themselves to God with complete devotion" and are to love for the neighbor what one loves for oneself.

I am a Christian. I believe there is one God, the God of Abraham and Moses and Jesus, who comes to us in three persons, Father, Son, and Holy Spirit. I believe Jesus is God's son, who went about doing good and telling us of God's love. I believe Jesus was killed on a cross and raised up by God from death to life. I believe that in Jesus there is forgiveness of our sins and the promise of heaven. I believe that Jesus wants us to love God above all and to take care of our neighbors.

Muslim and Christian. There are differences, for sure. But there is a bond between us: love for God and love for the neighbor.

When those who do terrible things to God's creation and to God's children say they are Christian or Muslim, they both lie. The truth is spoken for both the Christian and the Muslim when the apostle John writes, "Those who say, 'I love God,' and hate their brothers or sisters, are liars.

For those who do not love a brother or sister whom they have seen, cannot love God whom they have not seen." (1 John 4:20)

I am learning about Adnan's faith.

This I already know… we are friends.

~

100. Heaven

His Mom had died. The note he handed me read, "I want to go to heaven because I miss my Mom."

Is that not a large part of our desire for heaven? Would we be so anxious or agreeable to the prospect of eternal life were we to spend it alone? We have this hope that we will once again be reunited with those we have known and loved upon this earth. Parents will see their children and friends will pick up old conversations. Every tear will be wiped away, in part because we will once again be with those we have come to love on this earth. It is of faith, not fact, for sure. But it is a hope that sustains us and keeps us when we put our family and friends into the earth, ashes to ashes, dust to dust.

~

A Morning Word

O God, from my youth you have taught me,
and I still proclaim your wondrous deeds.
So even to old age and gray hairs,
O God, do not forsake me,
until I proclaim your might
to all the generations to come.

Psalm 71:17-18

A Morning Prayer

Grant to me this day, O God,
alert eyes, to see all your children,
of every age. Help me to speak with
gentle voice, and grant me opportunity,
courage, and strength to give a helping hand.
Even as my body weakens and my senses dim,
make me useful.
Amen.

101. Empty

Take eat; this is my body...Drink from it, all of you; for this is my blood... which is poured out for many for the forgiveness of sins.

Matthew 26:26-28

It was Wednesday, August 6, 1997, my fifty-seventh birthday, the day I walked to the top of Mount St. Helens.

We got up at 5AM, left our camp at 6AM, and began the walk at 7:30. There were ten of us when we began. The first two miles was wooded ground and a gradual climb. After those two miles, my sister, Merna, and Vivian, who had not planned or prepared to go to the top, headed back to camp.

The next two miles was hillside, full of boulders two to six feet in diameter. We were climbing now.

The last mile, the most difficult, was ash and small rocks. It was like walking uphill on a beach. Our feet sank in, two or three inches with each step. A step forward, slide back... Another step, another slide back...

We were at the rim at 12:30 PM. It took five hours to cover the five miles from the base to the rim.

We spent one hour on the rim, looking into this vast, vacant valley, one mile across; a desolate, harsh crater with a lava dome in the center. The mountain was growing once again.

At 1:30 we headed back to camp. It was another five-hour journey, the most tiring, the most reckless. At one point we attempted to slide down on the snow. We were back at the base and in our cars by 6:30PM., and in camp by 7:30. We were empty.

When I got back to camp, I immediately drank a quart of bottled water. At supper I drank three cans of pop. After supper I drank another half quart of water. For the next 24 hours I had this great thirst and hunger.

167

My sister, who is not a big eater, had eggs and pancakes for breakfast and was still hungry. We needed to be filled again.

My friend went through a divorce. When it was done, he was empty. He found that scripture and preaching no longer fed him. Words had lost their meaning. He also discovered that the Lord's Supper was still able to nourish him, fill him once again. When he came to the Supper, no status was required, no excuse or explanation was expected. He knew it was okay to come empty. Our Lord did not invite him to come in any other way. So he came empty and was filled once again.

USGS image of Mount St. Helens
On May 18, 1980

~

102. Let the Water Do Its Work

When I wash dishes, I have a choice to make.

I can grab a plate covered with food stains or a pan in which something has been fried, and I can stand over the sink and scrub and scrub and scrub.

Or I can fill the sink with hot soapy water, place the plate or pan completely under, as if to drown it, then walk away for a while and let the water do its work.

God must have made the same discovery, for we are commanded to baptize. We are told to get under the water and let the water do its work.

God promises we can count on the waters of baptism to wash us clean. We can rest in the promise the water brings: We are forgiven. We are God's children. We have a home in heaven.

The water will do its work.

Or, we can scrub and scrub and scrub.

~

103. Greater

I have made my bed on Oregon sand,
heard the ocean's evening song,
fallen asleep holding stars in my hand.

I have walked on the outstretched arm
of Crazy Horse riding his sacred hills,
remembered how we did his people harm.

I have climbed to the top of a mountain
called St. Helens and stood on her rim;
saw a volcano giving birth once again.

Yet greater, by far, is this simple delight:
hearing the laughter of children
on a warm summer's night.

104. The Shape of the Cross

And this is his commandment, that we should believe in the name of his Son Jesus Christ and love one another.

1 John 3:23

The very shape of the cross is a grace to us. Two lines, one vertical and one horizontal, reveal our relationship to God and to one another. The cross is of one piece.

When asked which commandment in the law is greatest, Jesus says: "You shall love the Lord your God with all your heart, and with all your soul, and with all your mind. This is the greatest and first commandment. And a second is like it: You shall love your neighbor as yourself'." (Matthew 22:37-39)

The second is just like the first. They are bound together. We cannot separate them. They are of one piece.

We Christians do know how to fight. We fold our hands in prayer one moment and shake our fists at the neighbor the next, without considering the possibility that we could be just plain wrong.

Look at the cross. See what we did to him. See what we do to one another.

105. Lucas

Last Thursday, Lucas came into this world. He lives next door. And we who have met him have come to know that even though he has done nothing to earn his keep, nor has he brought anything to this world in the way of productivity, he is cherished and valued. He is fed and held, smiled upon and touched tenderly. People gather around him and are immediately filled with joy. He has not been successful or earned wealth, not given a fine speech or won a race, not run for office or taken up a cause. Yet he is loved.

His two brothers have already welcomed Lucas into their home and into their lives – no test to pass, no initiation.

"That's our brother."

His parents have no doubt that he is both gift and responsibility. Is he going to disrupt things? For sure! He will need almost constant attention for quite some time. He will remind his parents and his brothers he is only concerned about his own comfort and wants, and he will need to be taught to share, to wait his turn, and to look out for the welfare of others, including his brothers.

But before all and above all, Lucas is loved. Before he showed his beautiful face to the world, he was loved. While he is wailing out his desire to be fed or changed or held, he is loved. The greatest truth about Lucas is not that he will exhibit selfishness or that he will at some time fail or that he will do things that are not good or helpful. No, the greatest truth about this child is that he is loved.

Lucas is a sinner and therefore he will sin. Someday he may hit one of his brothers. He will certainly disobey his mother and argue with his Dad. He will do things that are not good or kind, but that is not his identity. His identity is not sinner; his identity is child of God. He is not, first of all, someone who commits sin, who does wrong; he is, first of all, someone who is loved. He is created in the very image of God and he is meant to reflect that image.

Genesis, the first book of the Bible, tells of our disobedience and rebellion against God, our pride and our desire to be like God, our jealousy, and even our willingness to take another life. But before that – when God first breathed into humankind the breath of life – we are told this: "God saw everything that he had made, and indeed, it was very good." (Genesis 1:31)

The way we see Lucas and value his life is the way God looks upon each child of God. In our Lutheran tradition we are quick to acknowledge we are sinners. We press home that truth by beginning worship with a confession of our sins. That is one truth about us, and our lives bear witness. But there is this other truth, this greater truth: we are made in the image of God.

We are loved, unconditionally.

Like Lucas...

~

106. It Seemed Like a Good Idea at the Time

I remember buying my first computer and asking the salesman how I should care for it. He gave some suggestions, then told of a gentleman who called for help in great distress. He had recently purchased a computer and it wasn't working. The salesman asked what he had been doing when it quit.

"Well, I washed the keyboard," said the man. "I put it in a sink full of water and now it doesn't work."

I am sure the gentleman thought it a good idea at the time.

Most things we do, we do because they seem to be a good idea at the time. I have never heard anyone say: "This seems like a really bad idea, so let's do it."

My sister Merna is retired. She decided to volunteer as a substitute teacher. We visited on the phone and she announced that the next day she would be teaching a room full of high school students. The day after she taught, we talked once again. I asked her how it went.

"I will never do that again," she said slowly, and with great conviction. I am guessing that when she volunteered, it seemed like a good idea.

In my first parish, I asked the church council to tell me if they thought there were things that I could improve upon. They proceeded to tell me. Why did I ask such a question? Well, it seemed like a good idea at the time.

We all do it. So perhaps we need not be too hard on one another when things don't go well. Who knows, maybe it seemed like a good idea at the time.

~

107. There is an End

When my father died, he had already given away most of everything he owned. After his funeral, we children sat with our spouses in a tiny living room with all his earthly possessions in the middle and divided up what was left. I kept his billfold and deck of cards.

My father understood and accepted the truth that there is an end.

When we are able to acknowledge that end, we are better able to live more faithfully and responsibly in the present.

We have all heard the stories of people who have been told they have six months or six weeks to live. It changes everything. Now we decide to get it right. Now we will fix the brokenness, heal the old wounds, bless the ones we love, have the conversation.

All of it.

We live differently when we know there is an end.

Three young siblings were fighting before bedtime, until the parents intervened and sent them all to bed. About 2:00 in the morning, a very loud thunderstorm erupted and Dad was concerned the children would be afraid, so he went downstairs to check on them. He found the beds empty and called out to his children. A high, scared voice responded:

"We are all in the closet, forgiving each other."

~

108. Easter

When the sabbath was over, Mary Magdalene, and Mary the mother of James, and Salome bought spices, so that they might go and anoint him. And very early on the first day of the week, when the sun had risen, they went to the tomb. They had been saying to one another, "Who will roll away the stone for us from the entrance to the tomb?" When they looked up, they saw that the stone, which was very large, had already been rolled back. As they entered the tomb, they saw a young man, dressed in a white robe, sitting on the right side; and they were alarmed. But he said to them, "Do not be alarmed; you are looking for Jesus of Nazareth, who was crucified. He has been raised; he is not here. Look, there is the place they laid him. But go, tell his disciples and Peter that he is going ahead of you to Galilee; there you will see him, just as he told you." So they went out and fled from the tomb, for terror and amazement had seized them; and they said nothing to anyone, for they were afraid.

Mark 16:1-8

Here is our hope . . . this beautiful and terrifying story.

Hope comes
after Good Friday,
after the cross,
after the death,
after the tomb,
after the silent Saturday.

Hope comes to sit beside
the sadness,
the loneliness,
the pain,
the anger.

Hope comes
because the stone has been rolled away,
because the tomb is empty,
because Jesus was not there.

Some say, foolishness.

I am
glad for such foolishness,
glad to believe such a story,
glad to have such a hope,
glad to be such a fool.

~

109. Three Years Looking at the Back of Ken Wagoner's Head

It was high school. We were seated alphabetically by last name—Vogel, Wagoner, Westgard, Wheeler. I knew this about Ken: he had great hair. I also knew he was not connected to any church, never had been. And I knew he treated everyone he met with respect and kindness. When he saw another human being in need, friend or stranger, he tried to help. When I was a kid, I don't think I knew anyone who was as good as Ken.

I have not had contact with Ken since high school. What became of him, I do not know. If the Church found him, invited him in, I do not know. If Jesus ever got his attention, that too I do not know.

But this is what I believe. Ken is one of those who will be surprised.

When Jesus finally says to each one of us: "For I was hungry and you gave me food, I was thirsty and you gave me something to drink, I was a stranger and you welcomed me, I was naked and you gave me clothing, I was sick and you took care of me, I was in prison and you visited me." (Matthew 25:35-36)

Then we will inquire, in turn, Lord, when was it I saw you struggling to put food on the table and I went out and bought some groceries for you?

When was it I saw you were new to the community and I went over and welcomed you? When was it I finally noticed you were living in poverty and wrote out a check? When was it I heard you were sick and I asked if there was anything I could do for you? And when in the world were you ever in jail, and I took the time to come visit you?

Jesus will answer: "Just as you did it to one of the least of these who are members of my family, you did it to me."

Ken only saw someone in need, and did not know that when he helped that flesh and blood person, he helped Jesus too. When he helped another human being, he got God at the very same time.

"When was it I saw you?"

Surprise.

We are also told in Matthew 25 that there will be others who will be just as surprised. Those are the ones who know all about Jesus, know all the stories from Genesis to Revelation, who may be able to tell you step by step how to come to faith, may be able to explain prophecy and revelation, but who seem to have forgotten that when you invite Jesus into your life, into your home, into your heart, he brings his family along.

Invite Jesus to dinner and he brings his hungry nieces and nephews with him, some with bloated bellies, who don't even look Jewish. Then he invites you to meet his brothers and sisters, who crossed over the border illegally, looking for a new way of life for their children, just like your grandparents or great grandparents did when they came here from Europe. Oh, and he also brings his cousin to dinner. She just happens to be a single mother, who doesn't always eat three good meals each day, even though she is working two jobs. She needs food stamps to survive and our government isn't interested. Then he asks if you might visit his Grandma who is dying and another cousin who is in prison.

And you say: "I don't even know these people."
And Jesus says: "They're family. They're my family."
Surprise.

~

110. Advent

Our grandson, Benjamin, is in love with his grandmother.
When he was five years old and he knew he was coming to our
house for Christmas, he marked the days on the refrigerator. He
was alert and awake in great expectation. He was full of joy at
the prospect of a promise being kept, that on a certain day in
December he would see his grandmother and it would be
marvelous and grand.

Advent is about Jesus coming.

Most people missed him in Bethlehem. Mary and Joseph
were there, of course, and a ragged bunch of scared shepherds.
Later some astrologers from the East showed up at his front
door. But that's about it.

Then he promises to come again, in glory. No mistaking who
he is.

Between those two advents, he comes into the hearts of men
and women and children all over the world by way of faith, to
calm our fears, forgive our wrong doing, and show us how to
live with each other.

His coming is always a good thing. Just ask Benjamin about
his grandmother.

It's like that.

~

111. The Way I Know... By Faith

Jesus said "I am the way, and the truth, and the life. No one comes to the Father except through me."

John 14:6

Imagine a river, deep and wide, that runs for millions of miles in both directions. Imagine a bridge that is near, enabling one to cross to the other side. There may be other bridges somewhere along those millions of miles, but I do not know of them, have not seen them. I do know this bridge and know it will take me safely to the other side.

I know the story of Jesus. I know of God's love through him. By faith.

I know this one way, this one bridge. Now, for sure, there may be other bridges, but this one way is the way I know. So I will stay in sight of this way and tell others of this way. For it is the way I know.

By faith.

I believe it is a good way.

~

112. She Waved

"Long ago God spoke to our ancestors in many and various ways by the prophets, but in these last days he has spoken to us by a Son, whom he appointed heir of all things, through whom he also created the worlds. He is the reflection of God's glory and the exact imprint of God's very being, and he sustains all things by his powerful word."

Hebrews 1:1-3

Vivian and I were in Maryland to attend the funeral of Vivian's niece, Nina. We stayed with our son, Josh, and his family, which includes our two grandsons, Benjamin and Finn. One day we went with our son and the two boys to a city park. There is a train there, which we rode, and a carousel. Vivian rode the carousel with the boys. Josh and I sat on a bench to watch and to wave as they came by.

Other than our two grandsons, there were only a couple of children on the carousel. One was a girl who appeared to be about three years old. She was on an outside horse, with her mother standing next to her. She looked scared, not smiling, staring out as if by not looking at her mother or the horse she was riding, she could pretend this was not happening. The second time she came by, I waved. I figured I could manage to wave to my grandsons and also wave to this girl without expending too much energy, so I waved as she went by. But she didn't see me. The third time she passed by, I waved again. This time she saw me, but I think she pretended she didn't.

When I waved as she came by for the fourth time, she still pretended not to see me. But when she came by for the fifth time, she waved back. Hesitant, to be sure, and still no smile, but she did wave. Then the next time, she waved and smiled. From then on, until the ride stopped, she looked for me as her horse came around to our bench, and each time she saw me, she smiled and waved.

I will never see her again. She does not know me and I do not know her, but I like to think that in those few moments it takes to wave, I filled her life with some extra joy. I know nothing about her except this, she is a beloved child of God, and this too: it was fun to ride that horse and even more fun to know that someone noticed she was riding that horse.

I am guessing I will not be able to find a proof text indicating that Jesus ever waved to anyone. But he did, and those to whom he waved knew he was paying attention to them, even for a few moments, which is what we do when we wave. It is only for a moment; it is so simple, so very simple, and necessary and important.

"Zacchaeus," Jesus called out to the short man up a tree, "hurry and come down; for I must stay at your house today." (Luke 19:5) Jesus was waving. Zacchaeus waved back. His life was different because Jesus noticed him, spoke with him, spent time with him, and welcomed him. Zacchaeus was changed for the better because Jesus waved to him.

Jesus said to the woman who came at noon to draw water from the community well: "Give me a drink." (John 4:7) I would like to think he said please, but we are not told that. With those words, Jesus waved. The woman was most reluctant at first, most reluctant, but Jesus kept waving; finally, she waved back.

One of the first things we teach our children is to wave: Wave at Grandma. Wave bye-bye. When Josh and the boys met us at the airport, as Josh's car came toward us, we waved, saying: "Here we are, do see us? We are here." Then to the boys in the backseat, we waved again. "It's so good to see you." When we left and our son took us to the airport, his wife, Lilla stood by the house as we drove away, and she waved. "It was good to have you here, have a safe journey, and come again." It is all said in that brief moment, in the raising of a gentle hand.

There are gestures in our society that express anger and frustration, but waving is friendly, an expression of kindness.

"It's good to see you. We hope you have good trip home."

It is so simple, so very simple. When two cars come to an intersection at the same time, one driver will wave to the other: "You go ahead." The other driver will respond with a wave that says "Thank you." No words need be spoken.

We wave hello and we wave goodbye. The wave is saying: "I see you there. We are on this earth together. We share this time and place. I care about you, and what happens to you."

Jesus waved. Jesus, the exact imprint of God's being. And so God waves...

"Here I am. I see you. I care about you, and what happens with you. Know that I love you."

And we wave back. "God, forgive me. God, help me. God, give me faith. God, thank you."

Sometimes, no words need be spoken.

There may be shyness on the part of some, a reluctance to wave back. You may need to wave at some people more often, may need to be persistent, but maybe the fourth time around or the fifth time, this child of God will wave back and maybe smile, and be changed.

That is the always the possibility when the one who is the 'exact imprint of God's very being' waves at you.

113. Because God Loves this World

In the movie *The Last Emperor,* the young child anointed as the last emperor of China lives a magical life of luxury with a thousand servants at his command.

"What happens when you do wrong?" the emperor's brother asks.

"When I do wrong, someone else is punished," the boy king replies. To demonstrate, he breaks a jar and one of the servants is beaten.

The New Testament gospels tell of God who reversed that pattern. "For God so loved the world that he gave his only Son." (John 3:16) Our faith is that Jesus died on a cross outside Jerusalem for our sins. And in that cross, in that particular death, there is forgiveness. When the servants erred, the king was punished. Grace means that the Giver has borne the cost.

Because God loves this world, your future is secure. Henry David Thoreau (1817-1862) was dying from tuberculosis. The year was 1862 and he was only forty-four. His aunt inquired if he was at peace with God.

"I was not aware we had quarreled," Thoreau replied.

Because God loves this world, your status is established. An Irish priest saw an old peasant kneeling by the side of the road, praying.

"You must be very close to God," the priest said.

"Yes," the peasant looked up, thought for moment, smiled, and responded. "God is very fond of me."

Because God loves this world, God's glory is revealed in the ordinary. God is there in the children fed, in the dishes done, in the comfort given, in the business conducted with integrity, in the seed planted and the harvest gathered, in the job well done, in the handshake and the welcome, in the patience of the parent helping with homework, in the neighbor helping neighbor, in the poor being welcomed, in the hug and the letter, and in the ordinary moments that the world might miss, but God notices.

It is often in the everydayness of life that we uncover God and God's graciousness, that we again and again discover God loves this world.

One of the reasons for gathering for worship is to get our vision adjusted, to see again, and to celebrate the God we have bumped into all week and maybe not noticed. We worship God who came to us in Jesus, who reveals to us his graciousness in water and bread and wine. For such common stuff harbors the very presence of God.

It is easy to become cynical. So it is good to worship in a community of faith on a regular basis, to be encouraged once again to praise beauty and truth, to be invited once again to be open to grace at every turn of life, and to resolve again to practice forgiveness on a regular basis.

Because God loves this world...

114. Waking From a Nap

It came to me in that moment of leaving sleep behind:
What will it be when I slip away,
when I close my eyes for that last time?
Will I hover over my family,
watch them in their distress?
Will I sleep with no thoughts at all,
no present, no future,
only a past I will no longer know?
Will I be raised up in a moment,
in the twinkling of an eye?
Will I see God face to face?
Is there something after this something?
But now I must get up and bake some cookies.

115. To Be Held and To Be Heard

When we gather in worship, it is in partly to experience once again the healing that comes from Christ as we make confession of our wrongdoing and our lack of doing, and receive forgiveness. And it is in part to encourage one another to not lose faith, to trust that we can be the disciples Jesus has called us to be, bringing healing and hope to those we meet in this world.

The church is, as it has always been, a communion of ordinary people, like you and me, living faithfully as best we can. If you are like me, there is a great sense of helplessness. We usually don't know what to do.

That helplessness is not unlike the helplessness of Jesus. For it was said of him, "He could do no deed of power there." (Mark 6:5)

A pastor heard of the death of a young man and went to the home of the parents with no idea what he could or would say. The door opened and the pastor blurted out: "I do not bring any wisdom; I bring my love and God's love."

People who are hurting usually don't want advice or explanation, but simply want to be held and to be heard.

We can do that.

~

116. Psalm 23

The LORD is my shepherd, I shall not want. He makes me lie down in green pastures; he leads me beside still waters; he restores my soul. He leads me in right paths for his name's sake. Even though I walk through the darkest valley, I fear no evil; for you are with me; your rod and your staff—they comfort me. You prepare a table before me in the presence of my enemies; you anoint my head with oil; my cup overflows. Surely goodness and mercy shall follow me all the days of my life, and I shall dwell in the house of the Lord my whole life long.

Psalm 23

I have repeated the words of Psalm 23 for more than forty years as I have stood before a casket held over the grave. The words come tumbling off my tongue. They are old friends.

I do not claim to understand or to speak all the words with absolute certainty. I have some fears. Evil does scare me from time to time. I am not always sure my cup overflows. I am not good with absolutes, even in faith.

The words are not magic, but they do comfort. They are words of trust and hope. There is a confidence in God expressed in these words that I do not always have, and perhaps the one whose casket I stand before did not have, but we desire it, long for it. So it is good to sing the words of this old song.

Maybe the words do not always express what is true in our lives, but they do express what we want to be true in us, and what we believe to be true about this one who shepherds us.

The words are a grace to us. The words point us to another, to the shepherd who desires that all sheep come into his flock, safe forever.

~

117. Discipleship

Uncle Jimmy was married to my Mom's sister, Emma. Jimmy smoked, as did many other family members when I was a child. One day Jimmy announced that the doctor told him to either quit smoking or lose his legs.

My uncle Jimmy had to change a lifelong habit because his life was on the auction block and he was being asked what he was willing to pay, how much of his body was he willing to spend on the pleasure of nicotine.

Jesus says in Mark's gospel: "If your hand causes you to stumble, cut it off... if your foot causes you to stumble, cut it off... if your eye causes you to stumble, tear it out." (Mark 9:43, 45, 47) Jesus' words are offensive, like the words of that doctor so many years ago: "Either quit smoking or lose your legs. Your choice."

But those offensive words say life is precious and we are given one life to live, and we can sometimes choose how to live that life. Choices do make a difference. Those hard words say something about what finally counts, about how there are some things more important than other things.

The doctor cared enough about Jimmy to say: "I want you to have life, I want you to live on this earth for a while longer, but if that is going to have any chance of happening, you will have to make a choice here. If you don't, then the choice will be made for you."

Jesus is also saying something about making choices.

Jesus says it is better to enter life maimed than to go to hell with two hands; it is better to enter life lame than to be thrown into hell with two feet; it is better to enter the kingdom of God with one eye than to be thrown into hell with two eyes.

The Greek word for hell is Gehenna.

Gehenna in Jesus' day was an actual geographical place, the garbage dump outside the city of Jerusalem where refuse and the dead bodies of animals and criminals were dumped.

It was a place where fire burned continually to consume all that garbage and death. To be in Gehenna was to be separate from community and from life.

Sometimes we choose hell. We decide to go to Gehenna. We decide to live as if we have no family, no community, no purpose, no responsibility for the other, no life, and no God.

It was also outside the city where the criminals were executed, where crosses were planted in the ground and people were nailed to the wood and left for days to die.

Jesus went there. He went to Gehenna. Even outside the community, in places of garbage and death, he can be found. Even there, in Gehenna, there is hope.

Jimmy quit smoking. I remember the pack of gum he would carry in his shirt pocket in place of that pack of cigarettes and how, out of pure habit, he would reach for that cigarette and his hand would come back with a stick of gum.

Jimmy chose life.

~

118. From a Different Perspective

I am sitting in the balcony in the United Church of Christ. We are gathered as an ecumenical community in Lent. I sit alone in the front row and realize that I recognize several people by seeing the tops of their heads. I wonder if this is how God sees us, knows us. I have this compulsion to reach down and rub all those heads, and by so doing, tell them how much they are loved, how much faith God has in each lovely head.

~

119. August 29, 2006

Today, in South Dakota,
we plan to kill a man,
the state, all of us, so
students in school
have the opportunity
for discussion, and over
lunch, between bites,
old men can debate
gas prices and lethal
injection, and a woman
questioned at the mall
says she wants to
be there to watch, but
a high school student
has homecoming
to plan, so hasn't
thought much about
this man who will die,
who did a terrible
thing, who killed
another human being,
and today we plan to show
this man how wrong
it is to kill another
human being, by
killing a human
being. Today, in
South Dakota, the
shepherd will leave
the ninety-nine in the
wilderness, go off
after the one which
is lost, and when he
has found it, he will
lay it on his shoulder
and cut its throat.

120. A Wedding Story
For Jeanne and Roy

I had been invited by the groom to be a part of the wedding service. This would be a second marriage for both groom and bride. Their spouses had died, their children were grown, and now their grown children blessed their parents in this new marriage.

I entered the church on that Saturday in September thinking there would be a small gathering of children, grandchildren, and great grandchildren, and maybe a few friends. The sanctuary was packed.

I stood next to the bride's pastor and the two of us spoke the prayers and heard the promises. I was also granted the honor of speaking a few words to the couple. Here are those words, as I attempted to imagine what these two might say to one another in the fall of life:

In the fall of life
you came to me,
when the days grow short
and cold covers the earth's crown.
I began to think of shutting up the house
in preparation for winter,
covering the windows,
closing up the spare room,
putting away the things of summer.
Then I looked up from my quiet work
and greeted you, my friend.
It was good in the fall
to make a new friend.
We laughed and we danced,
spoke of springs and summers,
the coming winter.
We talked of sadness and faith,
played like summer's children.

Remembering how good it had been,

it could be again.
With the wisdom of seasons lived,
love remembered,
we who had walked in cemeteries,
walked again in the garden.
Not goodbye to yesterday,
the love of lover past,
but fall is as true and good as summer,
as full of promise as spring.
We have the days to cherish,
even as summer's children
might wish them away.
Like the marigolds of fall,
their deepest color,
their strongest stand,
we begin together.
The Lord God blesses
with word and water,
with bread and wine,
with laughter and touch,
with memory and friend,
and the sweet kiss of fall.
For in the fall of life
you came to me.

I think it is important to tell you that the bride was eighty-four and the groom was ninety. After the wedding, they went on their honeymoon to the Holy Land.

I am pretty sure this little story of this one wedding will not change the world; my poem will not contribute to easing the world's ills. But I do believe you are smiling now, which is always a good thing. In a world where there are many stories that give us reason to be afraid or sad, it is a blessing to hear a story that causes one to give thanks and praise to God, to nudge the person next to you with your elbow and say:

"That's great! That's just great!"

121. When Beautiful Things Happen

Two stories:

First story. On May 6, 2012, George Lindsey died. He was eighty-three years old. Maybe that name is not familiar to you or maybe you know him as Goober, the character he played on *The Andy Griffith Show* from 1964 to 1968, then on *Mayberry RFD* from 1968 to 1971, and finally on *Hee Haw* from 1971 until 1993.

I tell you this because of what Andy Griffith said after George Lindsey died. Griffith said George was his friend. They were both in their eighties and were not afraid to tell one another that they loved each other. He said they would talk on the telephone often, and he had visited with George Lindsey just a few days before his death. The last thing they said to one another was "I love you."

Beautiful.

Second story. In the spring of 2008, there was a college women's softball game between Central Washington and Western Oregon. One of the players for Western Oregon, Sara Tucholsky, hit the first home run of her career. She ran to first, but missed the base. When she stopped and turned to go back to tag up, she hurt her knee and fell to the ground. She crawled to first base. Western's first base coach knew that if Sara received any assistance from her teammates or if the coach replaced her with a pinch runner, Sara's first home run would only count as a single, so he shouted that no one was to touch Sara.

While the coaches and umpires tried to figure what to do, Mallory Holtman, who was playing first base for Central Washington, walked into the huddle and asked if it would be OK if she and another player for Central Washington carried Sara around the diamond so she could touch each base.

With the umpires' blessing, Mallory and a teammate, Liz Wallace, picked up Sara and carried her toward second base.

Trying to figure out which was the good leg, the trio broke into giggles. By the time they reached second, just about everybody in the grandstand was on their feet cheering or crying. The game was won by Western Oregon, 4-2.

Cheer if you want.

In the New Testament, the writer of James gives this witness: "Every generous act of giving, with every perfect gift, is from above, coming down from the Father." (James 1:17)

Perhaps when a kind word is spoken or something good is done, when beautiful things happen, we could name it. We could say: "This is of God."

Jesus all over the place…

Grace is thrown out into the world, like a flower girl tossing out petals with great abandon, never fearing her basket will be empty, striding forward, eyes on the groom, a smile on her face, confident that right behind her comes the bride.

Full of joy…

The Gospel of John tells the familiar story of the wedding at Cana. Jesus' mother is there, as is Jesus and his disciples. The parents run out of wine. Jesus asks the servants to fill six stone jars, each holding twenty to thirty gallons, with water. The servants fill the jars to the brim. Then Jesus tells them to bring the jars to the chief steward for a taste. The water has become wine. The steward says to the bridegroom: "you have kept the good wine until now." (John 2:10)

Water has become wine.

Worry has become joy.

In the scheme of things, turning water into wine, even very good wine, does not seem to rise to the significance of making the deaf hear, the blind see, or the lame walk. And so it is that what most of us do each day, as servants of Christ, may seem pretty small. Yet no matter how insignificant it may seem to the world, it makes a great deal of difference to the one to whom you speak a word of kindness or lend a helping hand.

It is also a big deal to the God we serve. The small miracle at a wedding, the turning of water into wine, saved the honor of a family and bolstered the faith of some disciples. Jesus honors even a simple cup of water given to a thirsty person and declares it as worthy of reward from our Heavenly Father.

The Danish philosopher Soren Kierkegaard (1813-1855) once observed: "Christ turned water into wine, but the Church has succeeded in doing something even more difficult: it has turned wine into water."

Life can be difficult at times. The church should not make it harder. Better a small glass of wine, a little celebration, some laughter, some faith, some mercy, a bit of grace.

Andy Griffith and George Lindsey chose to say to one another: "I love you." Mallory Holtman chose to help someone on the other team. We make choices all the time—wine into water or water into wine.

We are the servants of Jesus who have witnessed this grand joke with eyes of faith. Water becomes wine, sinners become saints, and life comes out of death. We are able to serve an unseen God, the Creator of the universe, by helping the neighbor.

Beautiful things happen.

Jesus all over the place…

~

122. I Feel Sorry for That Old Man

Coming up these steps one at a time,
left foot up first,
followed by the right foot,
then the left foot up again,
followed by the right foot.
Like a child learning how to walk.
Now I begin to wonder,
how will he come down these
steps when the concert is over?
Coming down will certainly
be even more dangerous.
I feel pity for the old man,
yet anger too.
Why is he doing this?
Could he not have found a place
on the ground?
Why is he intent upon
climbing up and up and up?
So now, before you fall,
sit down for a while, please,
do not continue this.
You are scaring me.
But I do not know what to do.
Wait, there he finds his place
and sits, at last.
I relax, breath again.
Now what is he doing?
He gets up and begins to climb
to the top row.
What is wrong with him?
The lights of the carnival are below him now.
Yes, I understand, but still, why?
Now he starts down
and it is as I expected.

His balance is even worse now.
He sees his place, soon he will sit
again and I will relax again.
But he turns too quickly
and begins to fall, his hands
waving before him,
as if directing some unseen choir,
as if searching for someone or
something to hold him, steady him.
But he only grasps air and flails away.
Then, by some unseen grace,
he finds his footing. Steady now he
heads toward his wife who has not seen
his little dance.
The show begins, the music is loud,
but the old man is safe for the next
two hours.
Then I must ask myself,
how will I ever get back down these
damn frightening steps?

123. This is Our King and Such is the Kingdom

Christ Jesus, who, thought he was in the form of God, did not regard equality with God as something to be exploited, but emptied himself, taking the form of a slave, being born in human likeness. And being found in human form, he humbled himself and became obedient to the point of death—even death on a cross.

Philippians 2:5-8

Albert Schweitzer (1875-1965) once said: "I don't know what your destiny will be, but one thing I know: the only ones among you who will be happy are those who have sought and found a way to serve."

I was visiting with friends whose son is getting married to an attorney who just finished law school. My friends went to the swearing-in ceremony. The judge who spoke to the new lawyers said: "Remember, your task is to give a voice to people who have no power, no voice. You will speak for them and give them power, give them a voice to be heard."

We cannot comprehend the full meaning of the cross, how Jesus, the Son of God, would die for you and for me. But even though we cannot understand, cannot truly grasp this mystery, it stills us, quiets our troubled lives, and fills us with a hope, not in power or in wealth, but in God who serves, who "humbled himself and became obedient to the point of death."

There are perhaps two Easters. There is the one waiting for us, that morning surprise when we are raised from death to life, gathered to our parents, and put back on our feet in that place Jesus went ahead to prepare for us, where every tear is wiped away and death is no more.

There is also this Easter now, when we rise up to meet the day, hearing a benediction upon our lives. Maybe a little afraid, unsure, a bit worn, perhaps misunderstood by others, but knowing that in a world often enamored with that which is lie or fake, we have discovered what is real and true; we have discovered the grand secret of the kingdom of God.

124. Doing What She is Doing for Him

Truly I tell you, just as you did it to one of the least of these who are members of my family, you did it to me.

Matthew 25:40

My daughter, Christin, works with the Nebraska AIDS Project. She helps individuals and families who live with HIV and AIDS. The medicine that keeps her clients alive is very expensive, so part of her job is to make sure they can purchase this medicine and still put food on the table. If there are children in the family, she goes out at Christmas and buys gifts. She also meets with her clients, listens to their stories, and lets them know that she cares about them.

We are told in Matthew 25 that there will be a day when we will be judged; the judgment will not be based on worship attendance or the number of hours spent in prayer, but on how we treat the hungry and thirsty, the stranger, the poor, and those in prison. It seems it is all about how one responds to people in need. It seems we will be judged by our work. It seems that any talk of grace is missing in this scene.

Unless you speak with my daughter…

She would say that it is all about grace.

I was studying a text in preparation for preaching. The Gospel reading told the story of a leper coming to Jesus for healing. I wrote to my daughter and asked if it would be fair to compare leprosy to HIV/AIDS, in that both diseases are feared by society, both label the sufferer as unclean, and both cause the person to live in isolation. Here is Christin's response:

"I think it is a good comparison in today's society. Many people are uneducated about the disease, which leads to fear of 'catching' the disease. People don't want to offer a handshake or a hug to someone with HIV/AIDS. Most people I work with end up living in isolation and fear of others finding out.

"Some have not even told their families. I can't imagine living with this secret every day. I am blessed to be the person they can talk to without fear of judgment."

She confesses that she is blessed to serve. She is blessed because she makes daily life a little bit better for some who are treated as strangers by their own families, who are locked in a kind of prison, who live in poverty. Her work is a grace to her and she, in turn, is a grace to her clients.

This, too: it is the opinion of Jesus that what she is doing, she is doing for him.

125. Greater Works Than These

It was a Thursday, the last day of February, nine o'clock in the morning. I was planning to drive downtown and run some errands. Vivian was having coffee with friends. The pain began in my left shoulder and soon moved across my back and down my left arm. I could not remember doing anything that would have caused it, and assumed it would soon pass. It did not. At 9:30 I got in my car, drove about ten blocks, and then thought: "This is kind of dumb. I could be having a heart attack."

I returned home and called Vivian. She came and drove me to the emergency room at the hospital. By 10:15, I was having tests done, and at 5:00 that evening I was taken to another room where my good doctor took a look inside my heart. He found three partially blocked vessels, and by 6:30 I was back in my room with three stents in my heart. I went home the next day at noon.

There is a verse in the Bible, in the gospel of St. John, chapter 14, verse 12. Jesus is speaking:

"Very truly, I tell you, the one who believes in me will also do the works that I do and, in fact, will do greater works than these, because I am going to the Father."

As with so many of Jesus' words, I am not sure I understand what he is saying, but I want to believe he is promising that his work continues through us, and that the 'miracles' he performed are still being performed today. Science and technology are not opposed to faith or God. Rather they are gifts to us. And might it not be true that "greater works than these" are possible because Christ's work is done each day by millions of his followers all over the earth, not just in Nazareth and Jerusalem, and not just by this one who promised we would see "greater works than these," but by all who do good.

On that Thursday in February, one doctor and one nurse guided a wire into my heart, and watched as it ran through vessels that carried blood to and from that heart.

Then, finding three of those vessels at least seventy percent blocked, they put in three mesh stents, thereby enabling the blood to flow more freely.

There is another verse that I believe I do understand. It is found in the book of James, chapter 1, verse 17:

"Every generous act of giving, with every perfect gift, is from above, coming down from the Father of lights, with whom there is no variation or shadow due to change."

What I experienced that Thursday afternoon was science, for sure, but it was also miracle, a 'generous act of giving.'

A gift 'coming down from the Father of lights.'

~

126. Lord, Teach Us To Pray

*Pray then in this way: Our Father in heaven, hallowed be
your name. Your kingdom come. Your will be done, on earth as it
is in heaven. Give us this day our daily bread. And forgive us our
debts, as we also have forgiven our debtors. And do not bring us
to the time of trial, but rescue us from the evil one.*

Matthew 6:9-13

We say these words in worship, at weddings and funerals,
during Sunday School classes, as we begin meetings, and as we
end our prayers.

They are like an old friend whom we come back to often.
They bind us together as a community, connect us to Christians
around the world—Methodists, Roman Catholics, Baptists,
Presbyterians, Congregationalists and Episcopalians—all
praying these words, "Our Father in heaven..."

This particular prayer encompasses all we really need in life,
and brings us outside of ourselves. We do not pray: "My Father."
Rather, we pray: "Our Father."

We join in community, in a shared faith. We are not alone.

Jesus invites us to call on the one who was before all, the
one who created the rocks and trees, the skies and seas, the one
who will come to judge the living and the dead, the one who is
the God of Abraham and Sarah, Isaac and Rebekah, Jacob and
Rachel, Joseph and his brothers. Jesus invites us to call this one
Papa, Daddy, Father. When you pray, says Jesus, pray like the
child talking to her Mom or Dad. Remember that you love each
other.

When we become confused and afraid, when we are so
empty we no longer know what to pray, the words "Our Father
in heaven" come to rescue us. Many a time I have sat with one
whose memories are gone, who no longer knows friends or
family, not even the children who come faithfully to visit.

But these words are still there, a gift from God, so much a part of the person's being that when I say: "Our Father who art in heaven," the person will say the words with me.

Such a grace, this prayer…

Now, I do not understand the ways of God. There seem to be too many times when good prayers are not answered and I think they should be answered. Often I think God is either slow or wrong or both. But Jesus seems to be saying, keep at it anyway, keep banging on God's door. Maybe the banging is an answer. Maybe the very act of praying is a gift in itself.

Once, after our son was an adult living on his own, his mother said something to him that I have long forgotten. But it must have been a word of teaching or rebuke or correction, because our son responded: "You'll always be my mother, won't you?"

Quickly and sure, she replied: "You bet."

Does Jesus promise in this prayer, this beautiful prayer, that God will always be your heavenly Father?

You bet.

~

127. God is a Farmer

One of my memories of childhood was my father's insistence that trees be pruned. I grew up in Washington, our home sitting on two-and-a-half acres of land. My father began life as a farmer in North Dakota, so when he and my Mom and family moved west, he purchased dirt instead of concrete. Our house stood next to a wilderness of trees, bushes, blackberry vines and wild grass, on which he kept a cow for a time, then some sheep, and finally a couple of goats.

We also had fruit trees: two kinds of pears, three kinds of apples, two kinds of plums, and two kinds of cherries. Fruit trees must be pruned, and my father was a wild man when it came to pruning. He cut those trees back so far that it frightened my mother. She was convinced they would never survive, never produce another piece of fruit. But my father made those trees stronger and they produced more fruit.

In John 15:1, Jesus says: "My Father is the vinegrower."

The apostle Paul names the fruit God is growing: "… love, joy, peace, patience, kindness, generosity, faithfulness, gentleness, and self control." (Galatians 5:22)

Pruning is helpful, perhaps even necessary to produce such a crop. I am a better preacher now than I was forty years ago because I have experienced sorrow and disappointment; I have buried family members and good friends and have some understanding of grief.

My self-righteousness is pretty well depleted after failing many times. I have known some pruning in my life. If you have lived for a time, so have you. You have known trouble and defeat and heartache. It is not what you desired, but you have grown in your compassion and understanding.

There is a vineyard in Italy, owned by one family for several centuries. When asked what is key to raising grapes and making wine, their answer is: patience. One must be patient. When a new vine is planted, it will take ten years to produce grapes that can be made into wine. When that wine is made, it will rest in a cool cellar for many years before it is sold.

The vinegrower is patient.

Jesus says: "My Father is the vinegrower."

~

128. John's Christmas

In the beginning was the Word, and the Word was with God, and the Word was God.

John 1:1

When I was leading worship on a regular basis, the Christmas Eve service was usually hectic – children moving about and babies crying, a sanctuary full of people. Then Christmas Day would come and I would gather with a faithful few in the stillness of the morning.

Even the texts reflect the difference. The Christmas Eve readings focus on Luke's telling of the birth of Jesus. The story is full of people. The Emperor wants his tax money, so he orders all citizens to go to their ancestral homes for a census. Luke says the whole world is counted. When Joseph and Mary come to Bethlehem, it is so crowded that they can't find a room for the night. Add the shepherds who come crowding into an already small barn after the angels' visit, which includes a multitude of the heavenly host. Crowded, noisy, and hectic is Luke's telling of Christmas.

On Christmas morning, we let John tell the story. John brings us back to the creation of the world, to the stillness, the quiet of nothingness, the darkness.

"In the beginning was the Word."

Not words. Just one Word, bringing life and light. Then one man, sent from God, whose name was John. One voice in the wilderness with a single message...

So quietly does Christmas come in John's gospel.

Luke tells us of the birth of Jesus, and of the shepherds who come to bow down and worship this child.

But John invites "us" to hold the child and then tells of our birth.

"But to all who received him, who believed in his name, he gave power to become children of God." (v. 12)

I visited a mother in the hospital. Her baby was in her arms.

Would you like to hold her,
the mother asked. How
gracious, such trust,
to bless me this way,
her child just born,
placed in my arms.
Like God trusting us.
Would you like to hold him,
hold my son, gently, gently.
Hold one another,
gently, gently.

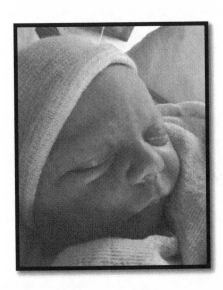

129. Crosses All Over the Place

It was early. My world was fog-filled and weary as I drove. I turned on the radio and heard a voice telling about the infant mortality rate in the United States. A young woman was being interviewed. She was poor. Four years before, she was pregnant and her husband was going to school. They had little money. She wanted prenatal care, but could not afford it. During the sixth month of her pregnancy, she felt sharp pains. She went to the emergency room...

In the middle of her story, I turned the radio off. I simply reached over and silenced her.

I didn't want to hear her story. I didn't want to become involved in her life. I didn't want to share in her troubles.

So I quit listening. It was easy. It's usually easy.

The hungry children look out at you from the printed page. Turn to the comics. Check the score. The poor are just statistics. Not real people living next door. Find something else to read. The guy begging on the street should find a job. Don't meet his eyes. Don't stop.

Look away. Walk away. Turn off the radio.

It's easy.

But the crosses are still there. All over the place.

~

130. God Has Called It

See what love the Father has given us, that we should be
called children of God; and that is what we are.

1 John 3:1

Consider the power of an umpire calling balls and strikes.
No matter what the machine might show on the television
screen, it is what the umpire calls that counts. If he says it is a
strike when the ball is actually high and outside, it is a strike.
The batter can mutter, the manager can run out and kick dirt, but
to no avail.

The umpire has the final word.

It is what he says it is.

God calls you child of God, and so you are. You might wish
to argue the point at times, knowing you have failed, knowing
you have acted as if you have no loving parent, no siblings or
neighbors in your care, but no matter, you are God's child. God
has called it and it is so.

Get used to it. Give it your best shot. Live up to your calling.

Sarah Smith, ten years old, was going outside to play with
her friends. As she was going out the door, her Mom called out.

"I love you, you know, and remember who you are. You are
a Smith."

God shouts to us in Jesus:

"I love you, you know, and remember who you are. You are
my child."

God has called it.

~

131. Will Not Let you Fall

Love is patient; love is kind; love is not envious or boastful or arrogant or rude. It does not insist on its own way; it is not irritable or resentful.

1 Corinthians 13:4-5

My grandparents, Gunder and Selma Olson, were married for sixty-five years. I never once saw them running down a beach in slow motion, arms outstretched, the wind blowing through their hair, jumping into each other's arms. But I had no doubt of their love for one another.

I was forty when Grandma died, so I noticed how Grandpa took very good care of Grandma when they were older and she was weaker. A few years ago, after both of them were gone from this earth, I was walking one day and noticed a small grove of trees. The trees were old. I then saw these two trees planted next to each other...

She's an old tree, branches bare,
some broken. The ground below
receiving life that used to be.
One day she got tired and tried to
lie down, came to rest against
the tree nearest. Since the
beginning, they have stood
next to one another, deeply rooted.

214

I stop now on this road to listen.
I hear him. It's alright, I
can hold you like this forever,
I will not let you fall.
It is my grandfather whispering to my
grandmother when she could no longer
care for herself, and he kept her in their
home until she died, never left her alone,
never let her fall.

~

132. Safe

I will both lie down and sleep in peace; for you alone, O LORD, make me lie down in safety.

Psalm 4:8

It was my first bedtime prayer. Maybe it was yours as well:
Now I lay me down to sleep.
I pray thee, Lord, my soul to keep.
If I should die before I wake,
I pray thee, Lord, my soul to take.

It is a prayer of trust. No matter what, I will be safe in God's care. "Whether we live or whether we die, we are the Lord's." (Romans 14:8) Of course as a child, death was not on my mind. It is more so now.

There will come a day when I shall close my eyes forever to this world. I don't much like the idea, but I am promised in these gentle last words of Psalm 4, that I will sleep in peace. I will be safe in the hands of God who has promised that nothing, not even death, will separate me from God's love.

In my last conversation with my father, he said that he was tired of this life. He could no longer see much good in this world and his heart no longer knew gladness. All he wanted was to go to sleep and not wake up again. One day, soon after, that is exactly what happened. I trust he is safe with God. I trust I am too, now and forever.

~

133. A Trip to See The Mouse

In January 1978, when our daughter and son were seven and five, we traveled from Gayville, South Dakota, to Orlando, Florida, to visit Vivian's parents. One day we went to Disney World®, the Magic Kingdom.

We have six pictures to prove it.

The week before Christmas, 2010, Vivian and I met our son, his wife, and our grandsons, who were seven and five, at Disney World. We spent five days at Magic Kingdom, Epcot Center, Animal Kingdom, and Hollywood Studios. We have sixty-nine pictures to prove it.

We have a picture of our children meeting Mickey Mouse in 1978, and a picture of our grandsons meeting Mickey in 2010. Almost thirty-three years separate those images and Mickey has not aged a bit.

This time around we had breakfast with Mickey, Pluto, Lilo, and Stitch. The grandsons have autographs from Pooh, Tigger, Eeyore, Pinocchio, Goofy, and Buzz Lightyear. We heard the Lion King roar, watched Indiana Jones escape the rolling boulder one more time, cheered when Nemo was found, and listened to the Muppets insult the audience. Our grandsons received training to be Jedi Knights, with Darth Vader and two Storm Troopers looking on. We met a lot of magical characters.

We also met some magical people, real people. We visited with a young woman from South Korea, traveling to Wisconsin to see her boyfriend; she is torn between her desire to be with this man she loves and leaving her Mom and Dad behind. She also spoke of her country's fear of North Korea.

I sat next to a man from Mexico, an architect, who said that his country is at war with the drug lords; he is concerned for the safety of his children. We waited in line with a family of parents and children and another family of three brothers, all from Brazil, who told of their country's efforts to create a larger middle class, to close the divide between the rich and the poor.

Standing in another line, we met a wife and husband and their three-year-old son from England. I asked the young boy how old he was and he talked for five minutes straight, hardly taking a breath. We visited with two university students from Brazil, who were spending their winter break working for the Mouse.

We met beautiful people from different parts of the world. God created us in infinite variety. It has been said that diversity is the essence of creation. But whether from South Dakota or South Korea, from Watertown or Sao Paulo, we all share in the desire to be understood and treated with dignity, to be in relationships with people who laugh with us, weep with us, and will miss us when we leave this earth. We all long to be loved and to love, to not be afraid, and to live out our lives in peace. We are all children of God and therefore brothers and sisters. For a few minutes in the week before Christmas, I was blessed to get acquainted with relatives who speak with British and Spanish and Portuguese accents, to find out how things are with them, and to wish them well.

~

134. Salt and Light

You are the salt of the earth… You are the light of the world.
Matthew 5:13, 14

Jesus is not commanding us to be salt or light, or anything at all for that matter. Jesus is simply saying we are salt and we are light.

The value of salt is in its difference. Salt is put into something else to bring out the flavor of that into which it is put, to make it taste different, hopefully to taste better.

It does not take much. Just a pinch of salt. Too much, and it tastes, you know, salty.

It does not take much light to break the darkness. If you have a dark room and open a curtain to let in the light from outside, an amazing thing happens. The light outside does not diminish at all. The darkness does not in any way change the light, but the light does affect the darkness.

You are salt. You bring flavor to the world. You are light. You break the darkness.

The novelist Henry James (1843-1916) was asked by his nephew what he ought to do with his life, how he ought to live his life. Henry James replied:

"There are three things in human life that are important: the first is to be kind, the second is to be kind, and the third is to be kind."

~

135. Hope At the Hardware Store
For Paula and for Jim

It is spring.
I need help with my lawn.
It is full of dandelions and quack grass.
I go to the hardware store,
where the wood floor sounds like yesterday.
There I will find
(along with nuts, bolts, screwdrivers, and lawnmowers)
fertilizer and weed killer.
She stands behind the counter,
with her black hair and gentle smile.
I ask, do you know anything?
Yes, she says.
I need help, I say.
I tell her about my yard.
I tell her how I failed in the fall to feed the lawn.
She gently shakes her head,
smiles this gentle smile,
which is both a confirmation of my neglect
(my sin really)
and an absolution.
The smile says, you are forgiven.
She says, you can begin again, it will be alright.
I borrow a spreader for a couple of hours.
I go home and begin once again.
I bring the spreader back.
Jim is there behind the counter.
I ask about the woman
with the black hair and the gentle smile.
I tell my story.
She gave me hope, I say.
That would be Paula, he says.
She is just that way.
A blessing then upon Paula.
A blessing upon all those who give us hope,
whose lives are just that way.

136. Giving Thanks

Note: I was asked to pray before the meal at a community gathering during Advent. A musical program followed the dinner.

I invite you, whether you are Christian, Muslim, Jew, or one who wishes upon a star, to join me in giving thanks.

I invite you to not only give thanks for the food set before you and the music that will cheer you, but I invite you to give thanks for all those persons who, day after day, go about doing tasks that need doing and who receive little attention and perhaps too little reward.

So thanks to the butchers and bakers and candlestick makers, thanks to the persons who set up these tables, those who will soon wait upon us at these tables, and those who will take them down once again.

Thanks to the person who washed this floor, the one who cooked this meal, the one who will put things back, and the one who will take out the garbage after we leave.

Thanks to all those unnoticed and unheralded souls, without whom we would be standing around at this hour wondering why we are here and why everything isn't ready for us.

And not only thanks to God, but perhaps you will be brave enough and kind enough to say such a word to the one who serves you this evening, directly to that person, face to face, to him or to her. Remember the admonition of your mother who, when someone did something for you or gave something to you, said: "And what do you say now?"

It is such a simple thing.

Please join me in giving thanks:

God of all that is good and gracious, of all that is kind and forgiving, we give you thanks for the food that nourishes us and for those who have prepared it and for those who serve it and for those who sit at table with us.

221

And we give you thanks for those who will sing to us and thereby fill our hearts with joy. We thank you. And we thank you for this season of mercy and peace which comes to us in the cold of winter, for the child whose birth we celebrate, given to us so that we may hold God gently in our arms and learn from him to hold one another even so gently.

Amen.

~

137. Someone

The kingdom of God is as if someone would scatter seed on the ground.

Mark 4:26

Some years ago at a Good Friday service, I made a large box in the shape of a cross and placed it at the front, before the altar. As people entered for worship, everyone was given a stone. At a point in the service, I invited people to come forward and place the stone in the cross. The invitation was to let go of something—some guilt, some problem, some burden—leave it at the cross.

Most members of most churches are pretty patient with pastors, and so my congregation was patient with me. They came forward and dropped their stones in the cross box. Nothing was ever said. No one said it was a good thing and no one said it was a bad thing.

Did it make any difference? Did it have any meaning? I didn't know. I scattered a little seed. I planted, not knowing if there would be a harvest.

Planting seed in Jesus' day was not a precise endeavor. The farmer would take the seed in hand and fling it out. Some would land on good soil, some on rocky soil, some on the path. There are machines today that drop in one seed at a time at just the right depth, all regulated by a computer.

What has not changed is that the farmer cannot predict the harvest. The farmer plants and waits, not knowing what will happen with sun and rain, with wind and storm and hail. There is a kind of helplessness about the whole thing. And there is a kind of hopefulness about it as well.

There is only so much one can do. One cannot make the seed grow. One plants and then waits.

The kingdom of God is like that.

We plant the seed, we speak the word or do the deed that is from God, is a grace to people, that lifts up or reaches out to another, and then trust that God can make it grow.

Martin Luther once said: "While I drink a little glass of Wittenburg beer the gospel runs its course." Helmut Thielicke (1908-1986) said about that statement from Luther: "That is truly the finest and most comforting thing I have ever heard said about beer."

Luther is saying: It is not me. I preach the gospel. I plant the seed, but then it is not me. God will bring forth, the gospel will run its course. The seed, so small it seems insignificant, unimportant, yet it will grow.

"The kingdom of God is as if someone would scatter seed on the ground." That 'someone' is you and me. We are the someone who scatters seed, who speaks a word of encouragement, who does the right thing, who listens or gives a helping hand, who in many and various ways lives out the kingdom of God each day.

A woman told the story of her father, who was a pastor. A couple came to his home with a child, asking that he baptize the baby. They had no connection with any church. They seemed to have no understanding of faith or their responsibility, but they thought they should have their baby baptized. The pastor baptized the child, all the time wondering if he should be doing such a thing since the parents seemed to have no understanding of the sacrament. He wondered about it for years.

One day, many years later, a young woman came to the pastor, reminded him of that time long ago, and said, "I am that child. I am a Christian." A seed was scattered and there was a harvest.

A woman came to church one Sunday. Her husband had died the week before, the funeral was just the day before, and she was almost afraid to come to church for fear of falling apart. But she did come. When she entered, she found that everyone there was also afraid—afraid to speak a word, afraid to do anything—until one woman saw her, went to her, wrapped her arms around her, and wept with her.

No words are needed. It is a small thing. It does not change what has happened. But in the midst of the sadness and pain, there is this sign. You are not in this alone.

Our Lord speaks to us a word of hope: faithfully plant and there will be a harvest. But there is also a kind of helplessness about it, for we do not know what will come of our planting. We do know it cannot be worried along. Obey and trust. Plant and pray.

Jesus says: "The earth produces of itself." (v. 28)

Luther said the kingdom of God is hidden in bread and wine and water, hidden in the ordinary, hidden even in a small seed planted faithfully.

I retired in 2004. In May of 2006, my good friend Jim died. He had been a member of Grace Lutheran Church in Watertown, where I served from 1995 to 2004.

After Jim died, I received a note from his wife: "Do you remember the time in church when we each got a little stone and put it in a box. With that rock we also put in a care or something that we couldn't let go of?" She continued: "You will never know how much that helped Jim with a problem he was having. We both thank you for that."

We never know.

We plant and we pray, and sometimes…

~

138. Startled

Then Jesus told his disciples, "If any want to become my followers, let them deny themselves and take up their cross and follow me."

Matthew 16:24

We took our two grandsons, Benjamin and the Mighty Finn, to the zoo.

Driving to the zoo, we passed a large carved wooden bear. At the zoo entrance, we saw another statue of a bear.

Now, at the zoo, Finn is walking ahead. He goes around a corner alone. We hear a scream. He comes running back, shouting, "It moved!" We follow him around the corner. In a cage, there is a bear. Moving, of course. Up until that moment, bears did not move.

Jesus, our king, says, take up your cross and follow me.

Up until that point, it seemed easy enough. Now we have something new to contend with. The bear moved.

Have you ever said: "I will never forgive him for that; no way in the world will I forgive him. I would rather die first."

Guess what? Jesus bids you come and die.

Have you ever held a fear or an anger or a hatred in your heart toward people of a different class, different race, different religion, different lifestyle? Have you ever thought, "I will never accept them. I will never welcome them. Over my dead body!"

Take a peek around the corner. Prepare to be startled. Jesus bids you, come and die.

It is fairly easy to love the world. It is people we have trouble with.

So which cross is it that will kill you?

That is the cross you take up.

~

139. Faith, Hope and Love

And now faith, hope, and love abide, these three; and the
greatest of these is love.

1 Corinthians 13:13

Faith
is fine as it is.
Do not confuse it with
another thing.
Let it be what it is.
A gift,
humble.
It must always love.
Such is its strength.
And fragile.
Doubt is likely around the corner;
tomorrow maybe.

Hope
is a cat,
comes to sit on your lap
when you least expect her.
Turns twice around
before she lies down
to bring her comfort.
Let her stay.
She may not.

Love
is best of the will,
more than the heart.
Better purpose,
than passion.
Better quiet,
than loud.
Better humble,
than proud.

227

140. To Talk of Spiritual Things

He was sick, sick unto death. We had just met. A nurse from hospice had asked me to visit him. We questioned and listened to one another. We talked of family and work and places and people and cancer. After a time, he said: "I suppose since you are here, we should be talking about spiritual things."

I thought we had been talking about spiritual things.

One's life, is it not holy? One's family and friends, are they not gifts from God? One's work, is it not a ministry? One's dying, is it not sacred?

God came to this earth and was born in a barn. He walked dusty roads and was buried in the earth. God wept, slept, bled, yelled, told stories, laughed, loved, was afraid and prayed, got hungry and thirsty, and died. Jesus talked of spiritual things like family, money, illness, marriage, religion, politics, and death.

Did I know what this man meant when he said: "I suppose since you are here, we should be talking about spiritual things."

Yes, I knew what he meant.

I wanted him to also know what I meant. The Bible teaches that God created this earth and all its inhabitants, and concluded that it was very good. When the Bible says: "For God so loved the world that God gave his only Son," (John 3:16) it means just that. God loves this world.

Jesus had lunch with a tax collector, resulting in changes in the man's tax law, and in turn, giving the taxpayers a break. Jesus went fishing with friends and his fishing wisdom got them a bigger catch, a boost to their economy. Jesus was invited to a wedding, where he changed water into wine, saving face and making the parents look good. These may seem to be insignificant deeds, except to those who benefited.

Jesus took the stuff of the earth, declared it his own, and gave it back to us, using water to bring us into the kingdom, bread and wine to feed us forgiveness.

Living in these truths, ordinary talk and daily deeds are spiritual things. There is no separation between secular and sacred. To look in the mirror is to see more than a reflection. We, with pimply face or balding head or crooked nose, are made in God's image. God will use us to do spiritual work, like taking care of our families, voting, sending money to fight AIDS in Africa, comforting a friend, making a meal for a neighbor, listening to Grandpa's stories for the umpteen time, or forgiving your stupid brother-in-law one more time.

Small, good things...

Heaven meets earth and earth benefits.

It's all spiritual.

~

141. He Will Rest in the Middle of Where You Live

When he first showed up at our house, I tried my best to shout him away. It didn't work. He wasn't pretty, but I guess that's the burden of most stray dogs. If they were handsome or pretty, they would be desired. He came plain and unwanted, in search of a home.

He was hungry. I fed him. He was mine.

He died shortly after he came to us. One summer afternoon he limped home, severely injured, crawled under the porch, and waited. A police officer came, the sound of his gun too loud in our small, quiet neighborhood. I didn't offer to help and I didn't ask where he would be taken as his lifeless body was dragged out from his safe place. I watched from a distance, sad and helpless.

He was a stray, skinny dog. I saw him just a couple of times, when no one else was around. He would sit a few feet away from the door of our house, under the shade of two old trees, like he had a home. He would rest in the center of our large yard, not like a stray, unwanted dog. He sat proud and beautiful.

Like a king.

No one else saw him like that or at least acknowledged such. I would like to think that at those times I saw him for who he really was.

There is a passage in the Old Testament, in book of Isaiah, which is a poem:

"He had no form or majesty that we should look at him, nothing in his appearance that we should desire him. He was despised and rejected by others… and as one from whom others hide their faces he was despised, and we held him of no account."

Isaiah 53:2, 3

The Christian church reads these words as a description of Jesus. Like a dog. Jesus came not with weapons of a warrior or

230

in the garb of royalty. He came as a teacher, a rabbi, born into a working class family, and he came looking for a home in the hearts of people.

The rejection of Jesus by the religious community, the betrayal by a friend, and the denial by one who was like a brother, are not only historical events; they describe the world's refusal to allow Jesus to get too close to where we live.

If you look with eyes of faith, you may see who he really is. He came from heaven, from the creator of all that is good, from the one who made you and loves you. Look with your heart, for Jesus will rest in the middle of where you live. Like a king.

~

142. A True Story

When they moved into the community and came to the church I was serving, they had been together for a few years. They came to worship, but never joined the congregation. When I retired, I heard that one of them was ill, dying from a cancer that would not be stopped. I would see one or the other from time to time, and ask how they were doing. It was difficult for both of them, the one dying and the one who could only stand beside and watch, and pray.

I heard about the death, but did not go to the funeral. Weeks later I saw Jim. We visited, had some small talk about work and weather, and then I put my arm across his shoulder and asked how he was really doing. He began to weep quietly, his head down, his voice soft, his words halting. He told me about his loneliness, how he had lost someone who really cared for him, someone who loved him unconditionally.

This story is not unique. You could tell similar stories of couples you have known, who love each other and have experienced the pain of loss. But this is a story of two men who are gay. This is a story of two men who lived together in family. This is a story of two men who loved one another, took care of each other, and did no harm.

This is a true story.

~

143. One by One
we are invited
to the Lord's Supper.
I am sitting in the second row,
so I can see them come,
one by one:
an old man held by his son,
a mom with a baby resting
upon her shoulder,
a child with both hands open,
a young couple, hands entwined.
I am blessed to
watch these beautiful people come,
one by one.
To receive with simple and profound faith.
Only to receive.
Nothing more is asked.

~

144. What is it You Want Me to Do for You?

James and John, the sons of Zebedee, came forward to Jesus and said to him, "Teacher, we want you to do for us whatever we ask of you." And Jesus said to them, "What is it you want me to do for you?"

Mark 10:35-36

They came to Jericho. As Jesus and his disciples and a large crowd were leaving Jericho, Bartimaeus son of Timaeus, a blind beggar, was sitting by the roadside. When he heard that it was Jesus of Nazareth, he began to shout and say, "Jesus, Son of David, have mercy on me!" Then Jesus said to him, "What do you want me to do for you?"

Mark 10:46-47, 51

The two brothers, James and John, ask of Jesus: "Grant us to sit, one at your right hand and one at your left, in your glory."

(v. 37)

Bartimaeus says to Jesus, "Let me see again."

(v. 51)

If you had to choose which of these requests to grant, what would you do?

Exactly.

Jesus seems to have thought the same thing. So you are as human as Jesus, or Jesus is as human as you.

The priorities of Christ's church are not that difficult to determine.

~

234

145. Thanksgiving

It is the least selfish of days.
The most basic.
We gather to eat,
and to be with
those we love
and those who love us.
We celebrate life.
We say thanks for family
and all good things.
There is no expectation of
gift or card or decoration.
It is not Jewish or
Christian or Muslim or
atheist or agnostic,
or it is all of the above.
It is as plain as plain can be.
A table, chairs all around,
the smell of hot food and
the laughter of family
and friends.
Of course we are
thankful,
and do we not wish
that all our days
could be as ordinary
as this.

146. Great with Child

Mary, his espoused wife, being great with child.
Luke 2:5 (King James Version)

Mary was great with child. What a marvelous phrase. It gathers together all God was doing into three words. Great with child.

This is how God came. A child. So we need not fear. Hold him close to your breast and to your heart. A child, waiting to be picked up, to be held and hugged, hungry for mother's milk.

Great with child. Even so, the words judge us as we continue to fight our wars, fill our homes with rage, allow violence to solve our problems, and turn our backs on the hungry, not wishing to see the children.

The first to suffer in famine and war; refugee camps filled with children, not understanding those they are told to trust.

Yet these words are our hope. Mary was great with child; the child we gather to worship on the Holy Night called Christmas. And we, like Mary, are filled with hope in this child, filled with hope for all the children.

Great with child. Such is God's word to us, God's promise to us. You need only have faith like a child. Jesus took a child in his arms: "Let the little children come to me, and do not stop them; for it is to such as these that the Kingdom of heaven belongs." (Matthew 19:14)

We will pray and we will work for the children who live in homes filled with rage and violence, the children with the wide, amazed eyes, lying in hospital beds wondering, the children with bloated bellies waiting for someone to come.

God came to us in one particular child named Jesus, so we will not be afraid of God and so we will not forget the children.

147. What If and What Then?

For God so loved the world that he gave his only Son, so that everyone who believes in him may not perish but may have eternal life.

John 3:16

What if it's all true?

What if a Pharisee named Nicodemus and a Jewish teacher named Jesus did meet one evening and have this strange exchange of words?

And what if the teacher is telling the truth, not just some symbolic truth, but flesh and blood truth?

What if there is a God who loves this world? What if this God came to be a part of this world, taking on our humanity, our flesh and bone? What if God walked on this planet? What if this Rabbi Jesus is from God, literally? What if God did become flesh and live among us?

What if there is a God and what if God truly cares about this world?

It is possible, of course, that it is not true. That is why we call it faith. But what if it is truth even outside of our faith, an objective truth? What if it is true, not just because we believe it or want it to be true? What if it is true whether we believe it or not? What if it is truth outside of our imagination, our wishful thinking, and our control?

What if it is true, these words from this Jewish teacher? Not true like the tooth fairy is true or Santa Claus is true, but truth as real as the pain you feel when you stub your toe or as real as the joy you feel when you discover you are loved.

What if it is true that God loves this world? Not just the Lutherans or the Baptists or the Methodists. Not just the Christians. Not just Americans. Not just white people. Not just the good people, the nice people.

What if it is true that there is a God and God loves the world, the cosmos, all of creation? What if it is true that this world, whether it knows it or not, whether it says so or not, whether it shows it or not, is loved by God? What if it is true that everyone you meet and everyone you have not met, everyone who has lived and everyone who will live is loved by God?

What then?

What if it is true, all of it?

What then do we do?

~

148. Let's Eat

While they were talking about this, Jesus himself stood among them and said to them, "Peace be with you." They were startled and terrified, and thought that they were seeing a ghost. He said to them, "Why are you frightened, and why do doubts arise in your hearts? Look at my hands and my feet; see that it is I myself. Touch me and see; for a ghost does not have flesh and bones as you see that I have." And when he had said this, he showed them his hands and his feet. While in their joy they were disbelieving and still wondering, he said to them, "Have you anything here to eat?

Luke 24:36-42

We gather at the church. Scripture is read. Words of remembrance and honor are spoken. The gospel is preached. Prayers are prayed. A casket sits before the altar. The sound of people crying softly can be heard, men chocking back tears, the whisper of children asking questions. Long periods of silence fill the room.

Then the slow procession to the cemetery, and again the words and the prayers and the sound of weeping. There is a reluctance to leave the grave, for now the truth must be acknowledged, as the body is left and the living return to the church.

And then... we eat.

Sometimes hot dishes, sometimes potato salad, or ham or turkey sandwiches with pickles and potato chips, or JELL-O®. And always there is cake and plenty of coffee.

It is as much a part of what we do as the gathering in the church and the journey to the cemetery. We eat. Laughter can be heard. The children no longer whisper. Babies are held up and admired. Hugs are given and returned. Promises to call, to stop by, to help, can be heard.

While the body is being lowered into the ground, the living come together to eat.

And it should be so. Because the living must go on living.
And because Jesus was living, he asked: "Have you anything
here to eat?"

It is a sign of life. It is what the living do.

It seems as if Jesus was always eating. The wedding at Cana.
With sinners and tax collectors. After teaching, he invited 5000
people to stay for lunch. On the night he was betrayed, he took
bread. Jesus was always eating.

But then, so are we. Important things happen and we eat.
Birthdays and weddings. A child comes home from college.
Friends stop by to visit. You have just been promoted. You are
going to ask her to marry you. The meeting has been adjourned.
It's the fortieth reunion of your high school graduating class.

We eat.

We are flesh and bone; we hunger and thirst for food and
drink, as well as for righteousness.

When God raised Jesus up from death to life, he raised up
his body. Then Jesus went to those followers who loved him
first, who had given him all they had to offer. For three years
they had listened to his teaching, trying their very best to
understand and be faithful. They called him Rabbi and Lord.
They watched as he was taken from them, and either ran or stood
by while he was hanged upon a tree. They took his body down
and left him at the cemetery. He was dead.

When Jesus greets these old friends, now afraid and perhaps
knowing they have failed, he says: "Look at my hands and my
feet; see that it is I myself. Touch me and see; for a ghost does
not have flesh and bones as you see that I have." (v. 39)

And then he asks, "Have you anything here to eat?" (v. 41)

Just like the old days.

God raised up his body. It is Jesus who is resurrected, not
just his spirit that lives on. So we confess as a church: I believe
in the resurrection of the body.

And then this marvelous sentence: "While in their joy they
were disbelieving and wondering." (v. 41)

The news is too gracious to believe, too good to comprehend.

The truth of it, the glorious, unbelievable truth of it…

And that is repeated every time we gather at the cemetery. We, too, are caught up in the glorious, unbelievable truth of it, and our tears are mingled with a faith that reaches all the way back to that day when Jesus came to his friends and said: "Look at my hands and my feet; see that it is I myself." In faith we now dare confess, and with our sadness and wonder and hope we proclaim: "If we have been united with him in a death like his, we will certainly be united with him in a resurrection like his." (Romans 6:5)

What joy it is to say: "Jesus is risen. He is risen indeed."

But that faith is not only for the cemetery. Such faith proclaims that Jesus is with us in our daily and common living, as much a part of our lives as the wind that blows in South Dakota: constant, sometimes obnoxious and troublesome. For Jesus will not let us miss the neighbor or ignore the children. He will not let us forget the poor or send the hungry away. As the wind is a part of our daily being, constant and troubling, yet cooling our fevered lives, so he lives, still constant and troubling, still teaching and forgiving, even leading us to places we don't wish to go.

Shalom, Jesus says. Peace be with you. No door, no sin, will keep him out. He comes with his arms open and forgiving.

Shalom, Jesus says. Do not be afraid of life. Live each day, fully, lovingly, with passion and with grace, finding the neighbor. Do not be afraid of death. "Look at my hands and my feet; see that it is I myself."

Then maybe, just maybe, to get those scared disciples to relax a bit, he asks, Oh by the way, do you have anything here to eat? And in truth, the question does startle, and in the end, it also comforts.

There is a kind of peace, a shalom, when we sit at table together. And he will join us. Do we not pray often, "Come Lord Jesus, be our guest"?

241

149. Preparation

When I was a child and our family knew that Grandma and Grandpa were coming, we always put the playing cards away and Dad put his beer out of sight.

A woman said that when company was coming in the evening, she would light candles all over the house and turn off most of the lights. She said it was beautiful, romantic, stylish, but mainly it hid the dust.

Our lives are lived between two comings, two Advents. We live after our Savior's birth in Bethlehem and before his appearing "to judge the living and the dead."

When John the Baptist told the people that their Messiah was coming, he was asked what they should do to prepare for his coming. John answered: "Whoever has two coats must share with anyone who has none; and whoever has food must do likewise." (Luke 3:11)

To the tax collectors, John said: "Collect no more than the amount prescribed for you." (v. 13)

And to the soldiers, John said: "Do not extort money from anyone by threats or false accusation, and be satisfied with your wages." (v. 14)

If we were to ask that question today: "What should we do to prepare for our Lord's coming?" John might say…

Parents, spend time with your children. Show them and tell them that they are loved. Do not destroy their hopes and dreams. Play with them and listen to them. Be the parent.

Children, respect your parents. Listen to them because they know more than you know. Don't talk back, and say thanks often.

Teachers, instruct each child not only what's in books, but also about life, about dignity and respect and kindness. Teach them about making wise choices, and show them how to live healthy, good, productive lives.

Politicans, don't take advantage of your power and your position. Listen to the least powerful in your midst. Be honest, be courageous, and be kind.

Pastors, love your people. Tell them of God's love and forgive them as Jesus forgives. Encourage them and teach them to watch for God in the ordinary.

Workers, give an honest and fair day's work. Do your job to the best of your ability.

Employers, pay a fair wage, so the person working for you can care for his or her family. Treat your workers with dignity and respect. Don't take advantage and look out for their future and their families.

Husbands and wives, treat your spouse with honor and affection. Remember the promises you made. Work as hard on your marriage as your job. Listen, listen, listen…

What should we do as we wait for the coming of our Lord?

I think maybe we live out our lives as best we can, loving God and loving the neighbor. We trust in John's promise, that the one who will come after John is more powerful than John. He is able to get into our hearts, and finally, with grace and power, separate out all the chaff, all the falseness in our lives, and gather us home.

Finally, we are made clean by the one in whom we are baptized. For try as we may, as best we can, we still fail and fall short. So in the end, John's admonitions will not save us, good as they are and try as we may. We need one more powerful, who is able to separate out the false and keep only the truth of our lives.

In the end, we are still children and we need someone to hold us, nourish us, pick us up, and carry us home, or we will never get home. And Jesus is able to do just that.

~

150. What's In a Name?

*An angel of the Lord appeared to him in a dream and said,
"Joseph, son of David, do not be afraid to take Mary as your
wife... She will bear a son, and you are to name him Jesus."*

Matthew 1:20-21

Jesus.

The church gathers in that name, has a mission and does
ministry in that name, sets priorities, makes decisions, and
spends money in that name.

What connects us as Christians, what binds us together and
breaks down the barriers between us, what unites us, claims us,
holds us, and comforts us is that name.

At home in my study there are memories all around, pictures
and books and ancient relics from my childhood. They are
important to me. But there will come a day when I leave them
behind and they will belong to another.

So what do I get to take with me? I will have my name, my
good name. When all else fades, when all else no longer matters,
I will still have my name.

And when your time on this earth is done, you will have
your name, your good name that means something, stands for
something.

When your family and friends gather to comfort one another
at the cemetery, they will speak your name and weep.

A good name.

An honorable name.

A memorable name.

But another name will also be spoken.

Jesus.

That name is joined to your name and that name dares to
give us hope. What you have when your world slips away, when
someone else gets all your toys, are two names: your name and
his name.

It is enough.

A Morning Word

Therefore I tell you, do not worry about your life,
what you will eat or what you will drink,
or about your body, what you will wear.
Is not life more than food, and the body more than clothing?
Look at the birds of the air;
they neither sow nor reap nor gather
into barns, and yet your heavenly Father feeds them.
Are you not of more value than they?
Matthew 6:25-26

A Morning Prayer

Gracious God, give me a bit more faith to trust
and not to worry so much about myself.
Teach me to notice others, to see all the
people who could use a kind word
and a helping hand.
If I am prone to worry,
may it be about someone else today.
Amen.

151. A Hymn for Advent: In All Our Days

God whispered grace in Bethlehem, in mother, child and manger.
So quietly did Jesus come, midst darkness, fear and danger.

God comes each day to meet us still, in home, at play and labor.
Christ comes in word, in bread and wine, and greets us in the neighbor.

When we lay down and tears are done, and thanks for life is given,
we have God's Word that Christ will come, and bring us home to
heaven.

So Advent sings a song of hope in God who comes in all days.
God's faith in us to do Christ's work gives courage to us always.

The eve of Christ, we children come to find the infant Jesus.
A sign from God in heaven above—with eyes of love God sees us.

~

Text: Gary A. Westgard
Music: English Folk Tune; arr. Alice Parker
Hymn Tune: No. 691 in Evangelical Lutheran Worship

152. A Hymn for the Church: A Covenant

A covenant, dear Church, a glorious promise.
By water, word God births you as God's own.
Now sing Christ's song, God's children of the promise;
Sing bold so God need never voice the stone.
Come, gather with God's many sons and daughters,
To hear Christ's word and share the food of God.
With friends to weep and friends to join in laughter.
Faith anchored deep within the cross's sod.

A covenant from God, a glorious promise.
Hope for our world, peace from God's very own.
Forgiveness from the Rabbi of the promise;
Grace gentle love to break our hearts of stone.
Tell people faith to laugh God's holy laughter,
Watch for the child and listen to the poor.
Kneel down before God's wounded sons and daughters.
With outstretched arms, Christ's Church an open door.

A covenant, dear Lord, a glorious promise.
By water, word you claim us as your own.
Freed now to serve all people by the promise;
From death's fierce tomb you took away the stone.
You raised Christ up, and we will join in laughter.
Love has burst forth, once buried in the sod.
Marked with Christ's cross as sons and as daughters,
We sing Christ's song held in the promise of God.

~

Text: Gary A. Westgard
Music: Irish tune; arr. John Barnard
Hymn Tune: No. 778 in With One Voice

247

153. A Hymn Story of Jesus: Our Redeemer

Come, dear children, see the baby resting on his papa's knee;
see the stable, see the shepherds, see this child who sets us free.
He's our Redeemer, he's God's chosen one.
He's our Redeemer, he's our King.
See his mama, how she loves him; join me now, her song we'll sing.

Hear his voice there on the hillside, telling stories to the crowd,
speaking wonder, speaking mercy to the least and to the proud.
There's our Redeemer and our gracious Lord.
There's our Redeemer and our King,
raising up the poor and humble, like a bird upon the wing.

Gaze upon the ruined tree, friend, feel the wood against your hands;
touch his wounds and touch his tears now, touch the pain that sin demands.
That's our Redeemer and the Lamb of God.
That's our Redeemer, that's our King.
At this tree we touch God's mercy, saving all from sin's last sting.

Come, you women, in your silence, bowing down into the cave.
Smell the fragrance of a new life at the terror of a grave.
He's our Redeemer, tell the world he lives.
He's our Redeemer, he's our King.
We will join you in your witness; into darkness faith we bring.

Come, all people, to Christ's table, join the laughter in this place.
Eat this bread and drink this wine now, taste the sweetness of
God's grace.
Sing our Redeemer, sing of God's own Son. Sing our Redeemer,
praises sing!
As we are, we come, God's children, to the table of our King.

Text: Gary A. Westgard
Music: J. Wyeth
Hymn Tune: No. 807 in Evangelical Lutheran Worship

Amen

About the Author

Gary Westgard was born in Rugby, North Dakota in 1940. When he was ten years old, his family moved to Longview, Washington. After high school, he attended the Lutheran Bible Institute in Seattle, Washington and Waldorf College in Forest City, Iowa. He graduated from Pacific Lutheran University at Tacoma, Washington, with a degree in Literature.

After graduating from Luther Seminary, St. Paul, Minnesota, Gary served as pastor in Laurel, Nebraska, then in Gayville, Meckling, Vermillion, and Watertown, all in South Dakota.

Gary and Vivian live in Watertown. They have two children, Christin who is married to Dean, and Josh who is married to Lilla, and two grandsons, Benjamin and Samuel.

To order copies of this book,
please visit createspace.com/4483326